P9-DMQ-314

TALES OF
THE LOST
FORMICANS

Constance Congdon

BROADWAY PLAY PUBLISHING, INC.

357 W 20th St., NY NY 10011
212 627-1055

First printing: September 1990
ISBN: 0-88145-091-X

Book design: Marie Donovan
Word processing: WordMarc Composer Plus
Typographic controls: Xerox Ventura Publisher,
Professional Extension
Typeface: Palatino
Printed on acid-free paper and bound in the USA.

ABOUT THE AUTHOR

Constance Congdon's plays include: NATIVE
AMERICAN, which was most recently produced at the
Lyric Hammersmith Studio in London in 1988; NO
MERCY (published in SEVEN DIFFERENT PLAYS,
Broadway Play Publishing, 1988) which premiered at
the Humana Festival in 1985 and was subsequently
produced at the Berkshire Theatre Festival's Unicorn
Theatre; THE GILDED AGE, which premiered at the
Hartford Stage Company in 1986 and toured the U.S.
with John Houseman's Acting Company; an adaptation
of Mark Strand's and Red Grooms' book REMBRANDT
TAKES A WALK, produced at The Moscow Central
Children's Theatre in Russia in June 1989; and
CASANOVA, to be produced at the Public Theater in
the Spring of 1991.

Constance Congdon has been awarded a National
Endowment for the Arts Playwriting Fellowship, a
Rockefeller Playwriting Award, and is the first recipient
of the Arnold Weissberger Playwriting Award. She is
Resident Playwright at the Hartford Stage Company,
and is a member of New Dramatists in New York.

TALES OF THE LOST FORMICANS was workshopped first at River Arts Rep, and then received its first production there, after a second workshop at The Sundance Institute.

TALES OF THE LOST FORMICANS was then produced by Actors Theatre of Louisville starting on 19 March 1989, with the following cast and creative contributors:

CATHY .... Lizbeth Mackay
ERIC .... Jason O'Neill
JIM .... Edward Seamon
EVELYN .... Mary Bouchet
JUDY .... Jan Leslie Harding
JERRY .... Bob Morrisey
ACTOR .... Jonathan Fried

Director .... Roberta Levitow
Sets .... Paul Owen
Lights .... Ralph Dressler
Costumes .... Lewis D. Rampino
Sound .... Mark Hendren

This production was chosen as the U.S. entry in the International Theater Festival in Helsinki, Finland.

TALES OF THE LOST FORMICANS was produced by
The Women's Project and Productions, NY NY,
opening on 17 April 1990. The cast and creative
contributors were as follows

CATHY .... Lizbeth Mackay
ERIC ....Noel Derecki
JIM ....Edward Seamon
EVELYN .... Rosemary Prinz
JUDY ....Deidre O'Connell
JERRY .... Michael Countryman
ACTOR ....Fred Sanders

Director ....Gordon Edelstein
Sets .... James Youmans
Lights ....Anne Militello
Costumes ....Daniele Hollywood
Sound .... John Gromada

For my father, Ned Congdon

CHARACTERS

CATHY *(nee* MCKISSICK), *early thirties*
ERIC *(her son),* 15
JIM MCKISSICK *(her father), late fifties*
EVELYN MCKISSICK *(her mother), early fifties*
JUDY, *early thirties*
JERRY, *early thirties*
AN ACTOR, *male, younger than* JIM, *who plays the following roles:* HANK, TRUCKER, ALIEN TRUCKER, B-MOVIE ALIEN, *and* JACK

All ALIENS *are played by the human cast members.*

PLACE

A New York apartment (briefly)
A large middle-class subdivision somewhere in Colorado

TIME

The present

PRODUCTION NOTES

About the Staging and Style:

The staging should be relatively seamless, with the stage space shared by all the characters. Furniture and other objects in the world are minimal because they are artifacts.

With the exception of the actor who plays JERRY, the ALIENS are played by the human cast members wearing matching sunglasses. They are human in their demeanor, except that seem overly pleasant and solicitous. (The character of JIM is only effective as an ALIEN in Act One.)

The VOICEOVER speeches should be shared by the actors as ALIENS (with the exception of the actor who plays JERRY). They need not be hidden while they do the VOICEOVERS, although sometimes it might be interesting if they were.

ACT ONE

(As the audience files in, JERRY lies on the stage, in darkness, lit only by a hand-held fluorescent lamp beside him. He is looking at the night sky with binoculars. He's lying on a sleeping bag. The chair and table for the next scene are pre-set nearby. After the audience gets settled, the lights bump all the way up and three ALIENS enter. They are the actor playing EVELYN, the actor playing CATHY, and the actor playing JIM. [The ALIENS look just like the characters they play except they all are wearing matching sunglasses. This device will be used throughout to distinguish the ALIENS from the human characters.] Two of the ALIENS unfold a star map and the CATHY/ ALIEN finds a small dot and points to it.)

CATHY/ ALIEN: *(To audience)* You are here. *(As they roll up the map, JERRY gets up and exits, discouraged, crossing near them, dragging his sleeping bag and carrying his fluorescent lamp — he doesn't see them, but they see him. One of the ALIENS cues the music and Muzak-like "elevator music" is piped in. ALIENS exit, leaving the stage bare except for a chair and table, part of a kitchen ensemble, typical in suburbia, but dated by a decade or so. The chair is upholstered with plastic and the legs of both chair and table are of bent chrome. The chair has a hole in the back rest — a design element common to chairs of this type.)*

VOICEOVER: First item. A situpon. *(Aside, softly)* What? *(Back to mike)* Chair. Chair. For sitting. Sitting and eating or some other ritual. Goes with table...which we'll see in a minute. Note the construction. Forward legs *(Aside)*

— they call them legs? *(Back to mike)* Forward legs are
made as one unit, curving up to provide the rear of the
chair. Rear legs are constructed in a smaller curve unit
which fits under the seat and inside the forward leg
unit, providing a very strong system for the body
pads — cushions — and then the body itself. The wobble
that some of these chairs exhibit we attribute to climate
changes...or some other entropic reality. *(An* ALIEN
*enters and "shows" the chair — sort of like Vanna White on
"Wheel of Fortune.")* Care was taken in beautifying the
chair. The sleek surface of the legs reflects light except,
of course, where there are spots of oxidation. And this
surface is the substance *chrome.* We have several other
examples of that substance — evidently a precious metal
used as a surface to apportion many religious objects,
specifically the numerous-wheeled sarcaphogae used to
carry spirits to the next world. The cushions of the chair
are covered in a substance made to mimic the
epidermis of the sitter, but treated to hold a sheen
which is kept polished by friction of the buttocks
against the surface. The significance of the hole in the
back rest is unknown to us at this time. It was, perhaps,
symbolic. A breathing hole for the spirit of the sitter, or
even the ever-present eye of god.

(ALIEN *exits.* JIM *enters, a middle-aged man in work clothes.
He is wearing lipstick and has a bandage on his right index
finger.)*

VOICEOVER: Next, the table. Four legs — the hard surface
covered with geometric shapes — decoration or,
perhaps, a code?

(JIM *lowers head, face down, staring until it slowly touches
the table surface, stays there. After a beat, the table wobbles.)*

JIM: Hmmmm. *(He rests the side of his head on the
table — pressing it gently against the cool of the surface.)*
Ahhh.

VOICEOVER: The table legs also wobble — this leading us to theorize that perhaps both examples of the wobble phenomenon are not random but conscious built-in representations of the unreliable nature of existence for this particular...species.

JIM: *(To someone offstage)* I'm gonna finally fix the goddam toaster. Evelyn?

VOICEOVER: Wait. Reverse it, please. *(Pause)* Please reverse it — it's too early — something else goes here —

JIM: Nilava? Retsote moddag aw sif eelaknife annog mee. *(JIM reverses his movements very fast and exits.)*

VOICEOVER: There.

CATHY: *(To audience)* Why would I move back home?

VOICEOVER: This is right.

CATHY: *(To audience)* I mean, I have a perfectly nice home of my — wait a minute — *(Stops to listen to something offstage, then back to audience)* — anyway, it's a two-bedroom apartment, rent-controlled — *(Stops again)* Excuse me — *(To someone offstage)* Honey? Mike? Is that you? *(Exiting to check on "Mike")* Mike? Are you throwing up? *(Sticking her head back in to talk to the audience)* He's in the bathroom. *(Offstage, to "Mike")* I'm coming in. *(A beat)* *(Sticking her head back in to talk to the audience)* Bad news. Excuse me....*(Offstage, to "Mike")* What? You *what??!!* And she's *what???!!!!* *(Re-enters fully, talks to audience)* Life's funny. One minute you're married. The next minute, you're not. One of his students, eighteen years old, "Kimberly", plays the oboe, the baby is his. *(CATHY exits.)*

JUDY: *(From offstage)* Home!! I'm home!! Jason!! Jennifer!! *Somebody* help me get these groceries outta the car!! *(Enters and crosses, lugging bags of groceries, stops near her exit and speaks to audience)* Last week one of the neighbors ran her rid'em mower the entire length of the street, on the grass — one mowed swatch through eight or nine lawns — flowers, toys, garden hoses all mowed into teeny, tiny little pieces — looked like a party. Then she hit somebody's rotary sprinkler and it threw her off course, but she kept on going, her foot flat on the gas, screaming at the top of her lungs until she came to rest, violently, against a garbage truck. Her husband died last year — he used to do all their mowing. I — I — I gotta move outta here. (JUDY *exits.*)

VOICEOVER: They reproduce with difficulty.

ERIC: (*To* CATHY *offstage*) You hear me, Mom? Everything is completely fucked up! I didn't get the fucking divorce. It's not my fucking fault. And now my entire life is fucked! *Mooooommmmm!* (CATHY *enters and looks at* ERIC.)

VOICEOVER: They are grouped in loosely stuctured units called families. Ring.

ERIC: (*Picks up phone.*) Yo. (*To* CATHY) It's someone named Grandma. Wait — is this the Grandma we're supposed to live with? (*To person on phone*) Where is this place? (*Listens to answer — turns back to* CATHY) No. No fucking way. Fuck no. (CATHY *takes phone.*)

CATHY: (*On phone*) Mom? Yes, they all use that word. A lot.

VOICEOVER: The economic system is antiquated, but communication is excellent, in spite of primitive equipment.

CATHY: (*On phone*) Yes, everything is fine. He's excited about coming. Excuse me — (*To* ERIC, *sotte voce, handing* ERIC *the phone*) Now, for Chrissake be nicccccccccce.

ERIC: (*Into phone*) Whatsup, Grandma. (*Can't do it, hands* CATHY *the phone*)

CATHY: I'll call you back, Mom?

EVELYN: *(On stage, on the phone)* No.

CATHY: *(On phone)* No?

EVELYN: It's your father. *(JIM wanders on.)*

CATHY: What?

EVELYN: He's...different. I don't know...

CATHY: Should we still come home?

ERIC: This is my home.

EVELYN: Please.

ERIC: This is my home!

EVELYN: Please.

ERIC: *This is my home.*

EVELYN: Please. *(They both hang up.* EVELYN *follows the wandering* JIM *off as he exits.)*

CATHY: Eric, we *have* to go home. We are going home. *And that's final!!!*

ERIC: You're outta control, Mom. You need to get some fucking help.

CATHY: *Listen!!!* I am the mother!! You are the child!! I am in control here!!! *I am the adult!!!*

ERIC: Mom. There are no adults in this world. I just figured that out this year. And this boy's not going to live in any fucking suburb. No way. *(He exits.)*

VOICEOVER: No way.

(JUDY is standing, looking out over the audience's head, pointing out houses to CATHY.)

JUDY: Split level, split level, raised ranch—

CATHY: Those are new. Nice.

JUDY: Ten years at least. *(Beat)* Now that's a new one—a twisted cape. High dollar house—didn't catch on.

CATHY: That was our little hill.

JUDY: It was just leftover dirt from something else. It wasn't, like, a real hill or anything.

CATHY: So what did our side of the street do?

JUDY: Some new siding. Above-ground swimming pools. Trying to be, you know....*(Points at a house)* New garage. It's a kit.

CATHY: Really? Huh. *(About another house)* Boy, that lawn looks like hell. He used to keep it perfect.

JUDY: You don't know?

CATHY: What?

JUDY: Spread newspapers on the living room rug, lay down, and shot himself.

CATHY: Oh my God!

JUDY: Of course, it still soaked through.

CATHY: *(Still about the suicide)* Why?!

JUDY: He lay there all afternoon. Say good-bye to that wall-to-wall carpeting. *(About another house)* And over there? She never leaves the house.

CATHY: That was a showplace inside.

JUDY: Still may be. We'll never know.

CATHY: *(Another house)* The...boys. Those wild boys...

JUDY: Killed in Vietnam. Killed in a car wreck. And the other one's a lawyer.

CATHY: Mom never wrote.

JUDY: I thought you knew, or I would've—

CATHY: Yeah.

JUDY: Nobody writes...

CATHY: No. (*A pleasant memory of someone*)
Oh, whatever happened to Darryl?

JUDY: San Francisco.

CATHY: Is he still alive?

JUDY: I dunno.

CATHY: (*About the neighborhood*) Strange.

JUDY: Yeah, it's pure Mars. I had to move back.
I couldn't afford my rent plus the Reeboks. Mom's
alright with the kids. I mean, that's the way families
used to do it all the time. This is a nice place to live.
We grew up here. It's not the subdivision that's the
problem, it's the society. My mother and I... get along.
(*Long pause, waiting for* CATHY *to say something about
this—agree with her*) I mean, you're doing all right, aren't
you?

CATHY: (*Realizing that* JUDY *wants to hear this*) Yeah.

JUDY: It's only temporary. Until I get a better-paying
job. I think I'm gonna start at one of those learning
centers they advertise on TV—you can put it on your
Mastercard.

CATHY: What are you gonna learn?

JUDY: Radiology. I don't know about wearing all that
lead. Can't be good for you. What are you going to do?

CATHY: Something'll come up.

JUDY: Remember that little dog that was in love with
you?

CATHY: Oh, the humper.

JUDY: Why don't we call him up for Saturday night?
Boy, uh. (*Beat*) Actually, he's dead. They get kidney
problems, those dogs.

CATHY: (*Thinking about the suicide*) Why did he do it?

JUDY: *(Thinking about the dog)* He was a slave of love, humping your leg — his little pink thing reaching out...with no place to go. So sad.

CATHY: No, I meant Mr. Whatshisname. *(CATHY puts a finger to her forehead like a gun. JUDY moves the "gun" so that the "barrel" is in CATHY's mouth.)*

JUDY: Bang.

CATHY: Oh.

JUDY: Yeah, he meant it.

CATHY: But why?

JUDY: Seems so incredible to you? He wasn't happy!

CATHY: Well, who is?

JUDY: But in a house that nice! You know?

(JUDY exits. CATHY stays on the "lawn.")

(JIM enters as before, wearing lipstick, and puts his head down on the table, just as before.)

VOICEOVER: This is the correct placement. Thank you.

JIM: *(About the coolness of the table against his head)* "Ahhh." *(To someone offstage)* I'm gonna finally fix the goddam toaster. Evelyn? *(He exits, returns with the toaster, sits.)*

(CATHY enters the scene and addresses the audience.)

CATHY: *(To the audience)* I'd forgotten how small this house is.

(EVELYN enters, holding a dish towel.)

CATHY: *(To EVELYN)* What?

EVELYN: He's in the kitchen. He's just sitting there.

CATHY: *(To EVELYN)* What time is it?

EVELYN: Ten a.m.

(CATHY *enters* JIM's *space,* EVELYN *following.*)

CATHY: *(To* JIM*)* What are you doing home, Dad?

JIM: *(Pleasant, oblivious)* Hi. I fixed this damn thing again.

EVELYN: What are you doing home, Jim?

JIM: What's for supper?

CATHY: What you got on your mouth?

JIM: ChapStick.

EVELYN: It's an honest mistake.

(EVELYN *wipes lipstick off* JIM's *mouth.*)

(*Phone rings.*)

CATHY: *(On phone)* Hello. *(She hands receiver to* JIM.*)* Dad?

JIM: *(Takes receiver, then puts it to his ear)* Uh-huh?...
Hello, old buddy... Home... What?! *(Looks at watch)*
What??!! *(Stands, drops phone)* No. *(Starts to exit, looks at*
CATHY*)*

CATHY: What is it, Dad?

EVELYN: He's supposed to be at work! Don't you see?!
He's supposed to be at work!!

JIM: I—I don't understand.

CATHY: Want me to go with you?

JIM: To work with me? Why? It's all right. Doesn't
anybody think it's all right?! *(He bolts out the door.)*

CATHY: Dad—come back. Daddy—wait!

(CATHY *exits after* JIM.*)

(EVELYN *notices the phone receiver which hasn't been hung
up—she picks it up.*)

EVELYN: Hello? Jack?... He's left. He'll be right there....
No, he's fine. Came home to get Cathy.
She's...visiting.... I'm fine, Jack.... Bye-bye. *(She hangs up*

*the phone. She looks at the paper towel with the lipstick in it.
The toaster pops — it's fixed.* ERIC *enters in his jockey
shorts — he's just gotten up.)*

ERIC: Toaster fixed finally? Get some frozen waffles
today — okay, Grandma?

EVELYN: No.

ERIC: Jesus, I can't even eat what I want? *(Exiting)*
I don't get to live where I want, I can't say what I
fucking want to say —

EVELYN: What did you say? *(Exiting after him)* What did
you say?

ERIC: *(Offstage) What kind of fucking life is this, huh???*

*(JERRY enters, sits in the kitchen chair, and talks to the
audience.)*

JERRY: First off, they get a warehouse — doesn't have to
be all that big, say, about the size of a Safeway. And the
first thing they do is spray the walls and the ceiling flat
black. And then they bring in about thirty loads of
number ten gravel and they cover the floor with it. And
then a couple, three loads of retaining wall rock — you
know the size I mean — about as big as my fist. And
they sprinkle that over this base of gravel. Now you
know they've made some mounds here and there, so
the floor isn't completely flat. They hand some lights
from the girders and set up some big spots, and they
got a control booth in a corner. Then they bring in the
machines — the lunar lander and the L E M. And that's
when they set up the cameras, shout "action!" and
make a movie. Then they print it in black and white on
crummy film in slow motion and pipe it onto all the
television sets. And whammo — all the world sees a man
land on the moon and plant the American flag. I mean,
"Moon Rocks"? Really. And don't talk to me about

Voyager. They got a ride at Walt Disney World better than that. Think about it.

(JERRY *exits.*)

VOICEOVER: He loses three days — no — wait. This is the female bonding scene.

(JUDY *and* CATHY *are talking.*)

CATHY: The kids? Your mom?

JUDY: At the mall.

CATHY: A little risky.

JUDY: I wouldn't go near the house — are you kidding me? His apartment. Are you into this? You don't seem into this.

CATHY: Oh — *I love* it.

JUDY: Yeah.

CATHY: I *love* this.

JUDY: Yeah.

CATHY: It's too much.

JUDY: Yeah.

CATHY: God.

JUDY: Right.

(*Long pause as they both smile and nod*)

CATHY: We're talking the same guy.

JUDY: Right.

CATHY: The one.

JUDY: That's right.

CATHY: Amazing. Makes me crazy! Uh! You are my hero. You are definitely my *hero.*

JUDY: There's just one thing.

CATHY: What? What?

JUDY: *(Beat)* I said the L-word. *(Pause)*

CATHY: What?

JUDY: I said the L-word.

CATHY: No.

JUDY: Yes.

CATHY: Was he...there?

JUDY: Was he there.

CATHY: Are you sure he heard you?

JUDY: Oh yeah.

CATHY: What did he do?

JUDY: It seemed to throw him off rhythm slightly.

CATHY: Then? You said it then?

JUDY: I know.

CATHY: Boy.

JUDY: I know.

CATHY: Was there any discussion...later?

JUDY: Nope.

CATHY: An acknowledgment of any kind from him?

JUDY: Are you kidding? *(Beat) Are you kidding? (Beat)* It would've been easier if I'd farted, frankly. Oh God. Oh God.

CATHY: I know.

JUDY: It's just—been a long time for me.

CATHY: I know.

JUDY: I just sort of, like, lost it.

CATHY: I know.

JUDY: Oh God, what an amateur.

CATHY: It'll be all right.

JUDY: He heard me say it.

CATHY: He'll forget. Men have short memories. Particularly for emotional information.

JUDY: Oh boy.

CATHY: Don't worry about it.

JUDY: I'm fucked. I'm totally fucked. Can you tell me I'm not fucked?

CATHY: Maybe he's different.

JUDY: I wish I could take it back.

CATHY: *(To herself)* Oh my God. Starting from scratch.

JUDY: What?

CATHY: Nothing.

(CATHY and JUDY exit in opposite directions.)

VOICEOVER: This is where he loses three days.

(JIM enters and sits at the kitchen table, and stirs his coffee very carefully, completely immersed in this action. EVELYN enters.)

EVELYN: *(Ready to go)* Alright.

JIM: *(Pleasantly)* Okay.

EVELYN: Are you go to the ready store?

JIM: What?

EVELYN: *(Annoyed, as to a child)*
Are — you — ready — to — go — to — the — erstoe?

JIM: I — I —

EVELYN: *Yaagh!! Yaagh!!* Are you ready to go to the yaagh?

JIM: Alright!

(EVELYN *exits. After a long beat,* JIM *stands up and begins to look around for her.*)

JIM: *Evelyn?* Baby?

(ALIENS *enter and take his table and chair, so when he comes back to where he was sitting, everything is gone.* JIM *panics and begins to run around. Suddenly a pair of headlights appears right upstage from him —* JIM *freezes in their light. A loud diesel horn honk. A* TRUCKER *enters, having climbed down from the truck.*)

TRUCKER: *Whatthehelliswrongwithyou?*

JIM: Who are you?

TRUCKER: Are you *blind?!!*

(EVELYN *enters with groceries in a couple of bags.*)

EVELYN: *Jim!!* Good *God!!*

TRUCKER: Is this guy yours???

EVELYN: Jim — you were right there with me at the check out — I turn around and you were gone!!

TRUCKER: Keep him out of the street!!

JIM: *(To* TRUCKER*)* I'll be with you in a minute.

EVELYN: *(To* TRUCKER*)* We're sorry.

JIM: Nice truck. Peterbilt!

TRUCKER: *(Exiting)* Dickhead!

JIM: *(To* EVELYN*)* Where's my coffee?

EVELYN: Come on, Jim.

(EVELYN *exits and* JIM *starts to follow.* ALIENS *replace his table and chair, but not his coffee. He turns and notices his chair and table again, crosses to it and sits — the coffee is gone.* EVELYN *enters in different clothes.*)

EVELYN: Alright. What do you want to do today?
(About his clothes) Wait — didn't I lay out some clean
clothes for you? These are the same ones you wore
yesterday, Jim.

JIM: I can't keep track of my damn coffee. Isn't that
funny?

*(EVELYN gets a fresh cup and puts it down in front of him.
JIM puts his hand in it and burns it.)*

JIM: It's hot. *Owwwwwww!!*

EVELYN: *(In sympathy and fear)* Oh Jim! That's your hurt
hand! *(She tries to get him up.)* Come to the sink — I'll
pour cold water on it.

JIM: No. Every time I leave this chair, something
happens.

EVELYN: I'll get a washcloth. *(She exits. HANK
enters — he's a male relative of JIM's.)*

JIM: *Hank!!*

HANK: Jimmy!!

*(JIM puts out his hand — HANK shakes it vigorously and it
doesn't hurt. JIM looks at his hand in amazement.)*

HANK: How are you doing?

JIM: What are you doing here?

HANK: I'm collecting for the Sunday paper.

JIM: No kidding. Why?

HANK: That'll be three thirty-five.

JIM: *(Looking in his billfold)* I don't have it.

HANK: *(Whispers)* Get out while there's still time.
(Horn honk. HANK speaks in a normal voice.) Gotta run. I'll
be back.

JIM: That's what you always say. Hank? Hank!!

(EVELYN enters, dressed differently again.)

EVELYN: I was honking for you, Jim. Didn't you hear me?

JIM: Hank was here, Evelyn!!

EVELYN: Hank is dead, Jim. Jim?

JIM: But he was here.

EVELYN: Jim — the paperboy yesterday — you called him Hank.

JIM: The paperboy is Scott.

EVELYN: Yes, that's right. Scott.

JIM: Scott — I know. I know that.

EVELYN: The doctor wants to check your hand today — *(She looks at his burned hand — the same one that had the bandaged finger at the beginning of the play.)* Jim!! You took the bandage off again!! Dammit! Come on.

JIM: Wait.

EVELYN: What is it?

JIM: I — I have to find my insurance card.

EVELYN: I left the car running. Don't be long. *(She exits.)*

(JIM takes out his billfold and sits down at the table and goes through all the cards and the pictures. As he lays the cards out carefully in a row, an ALIEN enters and begins to pick them up. JIM doesn't notice — he's become too involved, distracted, looking at some of the pictures he's found in his billfold. The ALIEN exits with the cards — JIM turns back to go through them, notices that they are gone — pats the table where they were, looking for them. Sound of a car horn honking. The honking becomes a long hum. JIM stares ahead.)

(CATHY and JUDY are doing the L-Word scene as in the earlier part of the play — like the tape is running backwards. JIM exits.)

CATHY: *(To herself)* Cha-erks mumrf geentrats.
Dog eyem ho.

JUDY: *(Backing in)* Kab ti kate dluk I heewa I.

CATHY: Tner-rerf-fid see eebyaim.

JUDY: Tuff tawn my eem illet ooya nak. Tuff eelatote
my. Tuff my.

VOICEOVER: We've seen this.

CATHY: Ti touba eerow tnode.

VOICEOVER: I said we've seen this. And X-load tape.
It's a zoomer. Thank you.

(CATHY and JUDY exit, still in the backwards mode.)

*(After a beat, EVELYN enters, sits down at the table, and
makes a phone call.)*

*(In another space, CATHY and JIM are in the cab of his
pick-up. JIM is humming "That Old Black Magic.")*

CATHY: Where are we, Dad?

JIM: In the pick-up.

CATHY: I know that.

EVELYN: Hello? Yes.

CATHY: Where are we going? Where's the job?

EVELYN: This is Mrs. McKissick. The doctor saw my
husband last—I'll hold.

JIM: Out...out.

CATHY: Another subdivision.

EVELYN: Yes, we have insurance.

JIM: No. It's a—a—great, big place where you shop—

CATHY: A mall?

JIM: A mall. And we're putting in the — the — *Goddammit!!*

EVELYN: When does he get back from his cruise, then?

(EVELYN *writes something down.*)

CATHY: Drainage?

JIM: Right.

EVELYN: Thanks. *(Dials another number)*

CATHY: But you're the foreman. What are you running errands for?

EVELYN: Yes. Our doctor gave me your — I'll hold.

JIM: Jack — Jack wants me to.

EVELYN: Yes. Yes, we have insurance.

JIM: You hear something? *(He stops the truck.)*

EVELYN: I'll hold.

CATHY: No. Where are we?

JIM: *(Still humming)* I hear something — a humming.

EVELYN: Yes, we have insurance.

CATHY: A humming?

JIM: Yeah.

EVELYN: Yes, we have insurance!

CATHY: We've got to get Jack this pipe, Dad. Dad?

(JIM *has phased out, hums again.*)

EVELYN: Blue Cross. *Yes.*

(TRUCKER *enters. Suddenly, he notices* JIM *and* CATHY *in the pick-up. He stops immediately and crosses to them.*)

TRUCKER: Can I help you?

EVELYN: ALL RIGHT.

JIM: I'd like a large root beer. *(To* CATHY*)* What do you want?

CATHY: Dad— (To TRUCKER*)* We're delivering some pipe. He's the foreman of the pipe-laying crew.

TRUCKER: Oh shit! Not him again!

CATHY: Listen—this is my father.

TRUCKER: You letting him drive?

EVELYN: *I was just talking to somebody*—oh, sorry.

TRUCKER: You'll have to back out. The street is closed off.

CATHY: Yessir. *(To* JIM*)* Back out, Dad.

EVELYN: Something's wrong with him. He's...

JIM: What? Oh.

EVELYN: Confused or...

CATHY: We have to back out. Back out.

EVELYN: *Some*thing. He's not...

CATHY: We *have to* back out. *Please*, Dad.

EVELYN: Himself.

JIM: Oh. Oh. *(*JIM *seems to be having trouble with the gear shift.)*

EVELYN: Thank—you. *(They've hung up on her—she hangs up the phone and writes something down.)*

TRUCKER: Back this truck outta here!

CATHY: Reverse, Dad. *(Reaches over, gets the gear shift in)*

JIM: I got it—I got it. *(Gets it into reverse)*

CATHY: Press the gas.

JIM: Right. Right. *(*TRUCKER *exits.)*

*(*EVELYN *gets up and exits.)*

(A beat or two later)

JIM: Who the hell was he?

CATHY: Shouldn't we turn here, Dad?

JIM: What? Oh. Gotta get this watch fixed.

CATHY: What's wrong, Dad?

(JIM is humming, doesn't answer.)

(ERIC enters, throws down his books. CATHY crosses to ERIC. JIM exits.)

VOICEOVER: They study the words and lives of the Dead. These hold Great Meaning for them.

ERIC: Fucking stupid American History. Not even in English! Now, Mom, I ask you, I fucking ask you, what the hell good is this for me?

CATHY: *(Looking at the book)* This is in English. These are just parts of original documents, that's all.

ERIC: Look! All the fucking esses are effs! *(Reads)* "Feftember 19. He failed on hif courfe, and made twenty-fix leaguef, fince it waf calm. Thif day, to the fip came a booby, and in the evening they faw another, and the Fanta Maria failed Weft toward the fetting fun." No way. No way. Not this boy.

CATHY: Eric, you are not quitting.

ERIC: I hate the bus.

CATHY: But you took the bus in New York all the time. It's no different.

ERIC: It's a different bus.

CATHY: *Eric, you are not quitting school and I will not hear another word about it!! Do you hear me???*

ERIC: I'm not deaf. *(He exits.)*

(CATHY *sits and reads* ERIC's *history book*—EVELYN *enters, distraught.*)

EVELYN: *Where is God??! (She lurches through the space.)* Where is God where is God where is *God??*Where is He where is He where is He?? *Where is God??! Where is God??!!! Where is He where is He where is....* (She exits, still distraught.)

(JIM *enters.*)

JIM: Did your mother come through here?

CATHY: Yeah.

JIM: How did she seem?

CATHY: Better.

JIM: That's a.... That's a....

CATHY: Good?

JIM: Good. Good. Good. Good. *(He exits.)*

CATHY: *(Reading from* ERIC's *American history book)* And on this corf—course they sailed until after midday of the next day, until it was found that what they had said was land was not land, but only cloud.... *(Introducing the next scene, to the audience, as* CATHY*)* "Possible Explanation Number One."

(JIM *enters with blueprints and a field book*—he's *working on a construction site and knows exactly what he's doing. The* ACTOR *enters, carrying an incomprehensible metal object*—he *is costumed as a* B-MOVIE ALIEN. CATHY *watches.*)

B-MOVIE ALIEN: *(Approaching* JIM*)* Greetings. Your overlord said you could repair any object.

JIM: What?

B-MOVIE ALIEN: It is very fucked up. We are...kinda stuck. Old pal.

(JIM *takes the object and looks at it carefully.*)

JIM: *(About a part of it)* This needs to be machined better, I can tell you that.

B-MOVIE ALIEN: No problem. Way to go. Far out. My buddy. Give me some skin.

JIM: Do you have a — a — nevermind. *(Takes a small all-purpose knife-pipe tamper tool from his pocket and opens the "knife")*

B-MOVIE ALIEN: I don't understand. Put away your weapon. We come in peace.

JIM: You're not from here, are you?

B-MOVIE ALIEN: What do you mean? I am Earth through and through. I hail from Ohio.

JIM: *(Too involved in fixing the object to care)* No problem. Never — force — anything.

B-MOVIE ALIEN: *(Repeats it into a small recording device)* Never force anything. *(The thing lights up.)*

JIM: There. *(Hands thing back to ALIEN)*

B-MOVIE ALIEN: *(Into recorder)* There. *(To JIM)* What is your task here?

JIM: Oh, I'm laying some pipe over there.

B-MOVIE ALIEN: Well, this is top secret. Know what I mean, butter bean?

JIM: Oh, sure — I'm used to that. Corps of Engineers, you know.

B-MOVIE ALIEN: What's your name?

JIM: Jim McKissick.

B-MOVIE ALIEN: Thanks so many.

JIM: Hell, I never even seen one before. I couldn't describe it if I had to.

(ALIEN *places his fingers on* JIM's *head* — JIM *is instantly paralyzed.*)

B-MOVIE ALIEN: Forget. Forget. Forget. Forget. How many? *(Looks in notebook — can't find the answer — does a few extra to be sure)* Forget-forget-forget. *(He's overloaded a bit — burns his fingers.)* Whew! No problem. (ALIEN *exits with gadget.* JIM *looks blankly at his hand, then exits, nearly catatonic.*)

CATHY: *(To the audience)* And that night I had a dream.

(CATHY *sits next to* JIM — *they are in the pick-up again.*)

CATHY: Dad, where are we now? We're going around in circles.

JIM: It's the circle drives.

CATHY: Is this the way to the job?

JIM: *(Reading street names)* Kiowa, Iriquois, Quapaw, Huron —

CATHY: Where are we?

JIM: *(Reading street names)* Saturn, Jupiter, Uranus, Mercury —

CATHY: Dad — what's that ahead? Like a big wall of —

JIM: Dark.

CATHY: But it's daytime. It's noon!

JIM: We ran out of streets. (CATHY *gets out of the pick-up.*) Watch your step.

CATHY: Where are we?

JIM: This is where the mall goes. See?

CATHY: No, I can't see anything — it's dark.

JIM: They haven't put in the electrics.

CATHY: But what happened to the sky?

JIM: There'll be skylights. They're in the plans.

CATHY: Can we get out of here?

(TRUCKER *enters, but is wearing* ALIEN *sunglasses.*)

ALIEN TRUCKER: Perhaps the little lady would like to
see a map? (*He snaps his fingers and two* ALIENS *enter
with a large, clear drawing of a rock, a wall, and a large
arrow like you see on mall directories. They hold up the
drawing*—ALIEN TRUCKER *points.*) This is a rock.
This is a hard place. You are here.

JIM: Alright. Thank you.

(ALIEN TRUCKER *snaps his fingers, and he and* ALIENS *exit
with drawing.*)

VOICEOVER: Jim? Thanks for bringing the pipe. It's
about time, Jim. You're fired. Please leave the company
truck.

JIM: Alright. Thank you.

CATHY: (*To invisible* VOICE) What????!! (*To* JIM) Dad.
Dad? Let's get out of here!!

JIM: (*Cheerful*) Alright. Thank you. (*He exits.*)

CATHY: (*To her exiting father*) Alright? Thank you?
Alright? Thank you? How do we get home? Dad?
(*To the audience*) And I woke up and it was true.

(EVELYN *enters, speaks to* CATHY.)

EVELYN: I can't believe it. I can't believe it. You believe
in something and they just take it away from you—they
jerk it out of your hand like a toy—like a toy from a
baby. Years and years and years and years. Thinking
you're part of something and you're *not*. Calling him by
his first name—Jaaack. Christmas presents. Being nice
to Louise—Looooweeeze, *Loooweeze.* It's not her fault.
But I just always liked him better than her. I mean, are
we just, just a pair of boobs? I mean—are we just horses?

CATHY: What happened? Mom?

EVELYN: Don't upset your dad.

(JIM *enters.*)

JIM: Jack doesn't want me any more.

CATHY: Oh no.

JIM: I need to get the rest of my tools out of the car.

(*He exits.* ERIC *enters.*)

ERIC: (*Surprised to see them*) Whoooops! (*Exits*)

CATHY: Eric!! Come here!!!

ERIC: (*Offstage*) Why?

CATHY: It's *noon*.

ERIC: (*Offstage*) I came home for lunch...*money!!* I forgot my lunch money. Yeah! I'm — going — back — to — school! *Bye!!*

EVELYN: (*To* CATHY) Well, what are you going to do!! Just sit there?? He's cut school! He's cut school! He's cut school!

CATHY: I know, Mom. What do you want me to do? *Kill him??*

EVELYN: *Yes!!!!* That's what I would've done to *you!!!* I'm going to help your father get his tools...or something. *Look* at *me*. I'm doing *something!!!* (*She exits.*)

CATHY: (*To her absent ex-husband*) Michael, you sonovabitch, where *are* you! You jerk! You asshole! (*Notices audience*) Excuse me. I don't know — I'm much nicer than that, really. Excuse me. Excuse me. 'Cuse me. (*She exits quickly.*)

VOICEOVER: What they call community is, in fact, random habitational clustering, but those in adjacent dwellings are labelled "neighbors" and are treated with tolerance.

(A phone rings at JERRY's *and keeps on ringing until it stops.* JERRY *just stares at it.* CATHY *enters, looks at* JERRY.*)*

CATHY: Excuse me. I was ringing the door bell. I kept ringing the door bell. Six, seven times. No one came, but I saw you standing in here, so I walked in. Excuse me.... Sorry.

JERRY: I was watching the phone.

CATHY: I wasn't on the phone. I was ringing the doorbell.

JERRY: But the phone was ringing.

CATHY: Who called?

JERRY: I don't know.

CATHY: It was me. At the door.

JERRY: They hung up.

CATHY: I'm looking for my father.

JERRY: Wow. Are you working it out in therapy?

CATHY: No. I'm asking around.

JERRY: Wow. Sort of street corner psychiatry? You just blurt things out and take whatever answers people give you?

CATHY: I don't have much choice. I am dependent on what other people have seen, you know.

JERRY: Oh — wow. Like using the wisdom of the world. No bullshit. Other people's experience. Would you like something — ?

CATHY: He's been taking walks. He's wearing khaki pants.

JERRY: I love khaki pants.

CATHY: And a shirt. He's been taking walks for exercise and sometimes, he gets...confused.

JERRY: I know about that. Would you like something to —

CATHY: There's something wrong with this floor.

JERRY: — drink? I don't get company much, but I have a well-stocked refrigerator.

CATHY: I don't drink a lot of fluids.

JERRY: You should. I know. I'm a nurse. Have you ever had the feeling that something that's just happened has happened before?

CATHY: There's a name for that.

JERRY: Really?

CATHY: Déjà vu.

JERRY: I've heard that before! *(Gasps)* Wow.

CATHY: It's French.

JERRY: France. They know about it, too! See? It's all over the world! Things happen! Things happen!

CATHY: Yes, they do.

JERRY: Another world — but it's this world. I don't know, maybe it's the government, but why do we know these things, if they aren't true? Why do we feel, like, this force, unless it's out there or, maybe, right here in this living room?

CATHY: Why would this force be in your living room?

JERRY: Exactly! You know. You *know*. I knew you would. We feel things that disturb us — right? Right? But why would we *want* to do that? Why wouldn't we just feel the things that make sense? But nooooo, no, no — God forbid we should have a little peace of mind. If we had a little peace of mind, we might think clearly.

Noooo — it's give you something, take it away. Give you something — Oooops! Dropped it. Bend over and pick it up now. Are we good and bent over? Goooood. *(Mimes gleefully kicking someone in the butt)* Sur*prise*!

CATHY: Do most people understand you?

JERRY: No, but you do.

CATHY: Not that much —

JERRY: I want to show you some pictures.

CATHY: I don't think so. I really have to —

JERRY: *(Takes photos from his pocket)* Here.

(CATHY looks at them.)

CATHY: Is this Viet Nam?

JERRY: No, it's my backyard. Look at the sky, see?

CATHY: It's all marked up.

JERRY: You see them!! I knew you would. Tiny, little metal kites in the sky?

CATHY: You drew them in.

JERRY: No, I didn't.

CATHY: I can tell.

JERRY: We're controlled by aliens. And they're idiots.

CATHY: I'm going now.

JERRY: Oh.

CATHY: You need to find some friends.

JERRY: *(Afraid to move his mouth for fear aliens will see him talk)* They're making you do this.

CATHY: No, they're not.

JERRY: *(Little mouth movement)* Yes, they are.

CATHY: I have to go. *(She exits.)*

JERRY: *(Looking up at the sky)* I see you. *I see you.*
(Flipping the bird to the sky) How's *that?*

VOICEOVER: Hmmmm. There's that gesture again.

(JERRY exits.)

VOICEOVER: Next segment: An object may have many uses.

(JUDY enters with a large a screwdriver in her mouth. She is watching the street.)

CATHY: *(From offstage)* Judy! Hey, Judy! *Judy!!*

VOICEOVER: Vocal intensity is frequently necessary for effective communication.

(CATHY enters, sees JUDY.)

CATHY: What are you waiting for?

JUDY: The skateboard hoard.

VOICEOVER: Offspring are born without wheels and must acquire their own.

JUDY: I'm taking Jason's wheels. He won't use Jennifer's skateboard. It's pink.

CATHY: Sounds serious. What did he do?

JUDY: It's all about power, Hon. And they've figured it out. We never figured it out. We were stupid.

CATHY: It's so windy.

JUDY: Nothing stops them. Even rain. My Ex came by. He's got a new Corvette. And a new girlfriend. She's young. Of course. Her biggest problem is if her blow dryer shorts out. Nature uses us. When I think that if I were watching TV some night and this movie came on where a small head appears from between some woman's legs and then this thing that is all wet and bloody comes out, and begins to bleat, and there's this long slimy tube attached to its body that comes from inside this sobbing and amazed woman, I would run out of the room and lose my dinner. And then I would call up the TV station and say, "What the *hell* is this horror movie doing on TV where my kids can *see it!*" So how's the journal?

CATHY: I gave it up. I can't write about my daily life.

JUDY: Why? I liked that story about the ant.

(Sound of a far-off beat box approaching — with about three kinds of music coming out of it at once)

JUDY: Oh, Jesus.

CATHY: What's that?

JUDY: Jagger.

CATHY: *(Sees him)* Who's he?

JUDY: Brain surgeon's kid. He's the leader. He's thirteen.

CATHY: I hear the wheels. There they are!! My God, they've got a sail! They look like a big ship!!! *(Music is closer)* Who *are* they?

JUDY: *They are our children!!*

CATHY: *Who are they?!!!*

JUDY: *I don't know!!!*

CATHY: Is Eric with them?

JUDY: No, but there's Jason *and* Jennifer!

CATHY: That sail looks familiar.

JUDY: It's my mother's Elvis Presley bedspread!! *Jasonnnnnn!!!!!*

(JUDY exits, running. ERIC enters, crosses to CATHY.)

ERIC: *(About the kids on the skateboards)* Look at those little worms.

CATHY: Eric — I was looking for you.

ERIC: Yeah.

CATHY: Grandma gave me this phone bill. Look at these charges— (Reads) —"$35.12—New York—2:45 p.m. $42.10—New York—3:10 p.m." And this one just last week: $65.37—three hours and forty-five minutes.

ERIC: Yeah.

CATHY: Have you been calling New York City in the afternoon?

ERIC: Yeah.

CATHY: Are you out of your mind? The rates are sky-high then!

ERIC: I needed to talk to Todd.

CATHY: There's not a conversation in here that's less than two hours!

ERIC: We always used to talk after school.

CATHY: But not *long distance!*

ERIC: Hey. I'm a long-distance guy.

CATHY: This bill comes to almost two hundred dollars!

ERIC: Hey. I didn't get the divorce. I didn't ask to move here. I didn't make Grandpa sick or whatever the fuck is wrong with him. Matter of fact, I didn't ask to be born. You and "Mike" had all the fun when I was conceived. I was exploding. You think exploding is fun? Doubling and quadrupling and sixteenth-toopling or whatever the hell it is. You're a blob, you're a fish, you're some hairless tadpole weird-looking piece of flesh? Huh?

CATHY: Well, for your information, conceiving you wasn't all that much fun!

ERIC: Well, don't talk to me about it! Call Dr. Ruth. And if I can't talk to my friends, then *fuck this world*, you know? *(He exits.)*

CATHY: *(Trying to come up with a parting shot)* Well — Eric! You know.... *(Gives up)*

CATHY: *(To audience)* Eric. Possible Explanation. *(She watches the following scene.)*

(JIM is reading "The National Enquirer" and EVELYN is knitting.)

JIM: Says here that alien beings have been abducting young girls, having intercourse with them, and then returning them to society where they, these young girls, bear monstrous babies, fathered by these alien beings.

EVELYN: Hmmmmmm? Ouch!

JIM: What's wrong?

EVELYN: This aluminum is hard to knit. *(Holds up knitting)* Booties.

JIM: *(About booties)* Strange shape. *(Back to paper)* These alien babies grow up to look pretty much like humans but are monstrous in that they have no respect for anything, especially their parents. Or their parent's parents. They hold nothing dear, these alien offspring, except each other. *(He takes the newspaper and exits.)*

EVELYN: *(To the absent JIM)* Sounds too improbable. Why do you read that trash? She's naming him Fong Emo Six. It came to her in a dream. *(She exits after JIM.)*

(JIM re-enters, without the newspaper, crosses the stage, stops, changes his direction, crosses briefly, stops, changes direction, talks to himself.)

JIM: There's nothing wrong with me. *(He exits.)*

(CATHY and EVELYN enter from opposite sides of the stage. They meet at the kitchen table and the argument begins.)

EVELYN:

There's something wrong with that boy! All those years you've been sending those damn pictures — he looked fine! "Eric — fifth grade," "Eric — eighth grade" — big smile and all those thank-you notes. I don't think he wrote them at all — I think you wrote them for him. In the meantime, look at what he's becoming. He looks at me like I was from Mars! Does he appreciate his own grandmother? Noooooo. Of course not. And your friend Judy — *she's gone off the deep end*. She's a complete slut!! I don't know how her mother stands it. I don't know how we all stand anything. Am I the only one that sees that everything is going straight to hell? I talk, talk, talk, and no one listens. Noooo. I asked you to come home for your own good and because I wanted an *adult* to help me because things are completely *impossible, impossible,* do you hear me?

CATHY:

I knew it!! I knew it!! You wonder why I haven't been home — you wonder why we haven't come home to visit? Because I knew it would be like this!! You have no idea what my life is like — what it's like raising a child in the world today. I was a *peach!!* When I think of how *easy* it was for you, it makes me *crazy!!* For your information I sat him down to write all those notes. And do you appreciate it? Noooooo. Of course not. *You could have come visit!!* But no — you were scared of where we lived. *Great!* Makes me feel great! Makes me feel wanted! And Eric, too!! He looks at you that way because he doesn't know you. But you don't know him! And you *don't want to know him!* Can you see how lonely he is? Noooo. Eric was right. This isn't my home. *I gave up my home* to come *here*. Isn't that a riot? I don't know who you are, I don't know who Dad is, I don't know —

(At EVELYN's *line, "* . . .*do you hear me?" they both stop for a beat or two, then start back up. [*CATHY's *stopping line may vary —* EVELYN's *line is the only cue.])*

But instead, you go to work, come home, and only think of your own problems. See? See? That's exactly what's wrong with the world today! It's *me, me, me,* and to *hell* with anyone else! And *that's* why *Eric* is the way he is. *Who* are his models? Hmmmm? It's coming home to roost.

—anything. And *now* you, my own mother hits me where it hurts the most!! But, of course you would—you're my *mother!! That's what mothers are for! Go ahead!! Kick me!! In the stomach!!* "Come home, Cathy—please." So I fall for it. And what do I get for it?

(CATHY *stops.*)

CATHY: *Oh, please.*

EVELYN: Yes, it's coming home to roost. Believe me, the world got by when men thought only of themselves, but when women do, we're *dead, dead, dead!!*

CATHY: I don't want to hear it!! Judy's right, no one really gives a *damn* about who is raising the kids as long as they don't have to put in the *fucking* time themselves!

EVELYN: There's that word again!! *See!!*

CATHY: I never use that word. *See what you drive me to?*

EVELYN: I brought you into this world—I can drive you wherever I *want!*

CATHY: I didn't ask to be born! You and Dad had the fun when I was conceived! *(Puzzled, suddenly)* Wait a minute—

EVELYN: It wasn't that much fun!

CATHY: Well, call Dr. Ruth!

EVELYN: What are you talking about?

CATHY: I don't know!!! *(She exits.)*

EVELYN: What am I—invisible?? *(She exits.)*

VOICEOVER: They are fascinated by tools, however primitive.

(It's dark. JUDY *enters, wearing clear plastic goggles and carrying a small propane torch—she turns on a flashlight, revealing* CATHY, *also wearing goggles and carrying another small propane torch.* CATHY *and* JUDY *are trying to be quiet. [Real torches are unreliable on stage—the effect can work with small flashlights in torch bodies. Electric carving knives can also be used—with appropriate line changes.])*

CATHY: I don't know about this.

JUDY: He says to me—

CATHY: You talk to him?

JUDY: No. He was just standing in the hall.

CATHY: Your hall?

JUDY: My mother's hall—yeah, my hall, my hall...now.

CATHY: How did he get in?

JUDY: I don't know—he was waiting for Jason. Jason had his mirrored sunglasses.

CATHY: Jason's just a kid.

JUDY: Don't start with me! I can't pick my son's friends! I can't lock him up! Besides, you know as well as I do—whatever is forbidden, they love!

CATHY: So Jagger's in the hall—

JUDY: "Fire is real." He says to me. "Fire is real." The kid is heavy.

CATHY: I can't talk about kids anymore.

JUDY: *(About what they're about to do)* Come on—it'll get your mind off Eric. And everything. Ready? *(*JUDY *lights their propane torches.)*

CATHY: What a beautiful little flame— *(Sudden realization)* Oh my *God!* What are we *doing?* Oh my *God!!*

JUDY: No problem.

CATHY: No *problem?*

JUDY: It's all fiberglass. It'll melt like sugar.

CATHY: Are you sure this is the right Corvette?

JUDY: Believe me, I know this Corvette. I've dogged him in it for weeks.

CATHY: Are you sure nobody will see us?

JUDY: Make any design you want. Be creative.

(JUDY puts flame to Corvette body. CATHY watches, tries.)

CATHY: It's melting!

JUDY: *(Working away)* The way I see it, they fucked up in the Sixties, you know? They, like, took away all the values and didn't put anything in its place. You know — so, like, everything just — the whole mess they left — just started to coagulate like it would — I mean, the laws of physics apply to life — Carl Sagan or whoever — those PBS guys have shown us that. Anyway, it, what was left of society, just coagulated like bad pudding, spoiled pudding, you know, like when the eggs separated and can't be put together again completely right. So they make this globular pudding or sometimes it happens to clam chowder. Anyway, it must, like of *formed* and we're stuck with it. There's a piece of God and a clump of law and a lot of lumpy, fucked-up pictures and words that don't hardly mean anything any more. And — ahh — I made a peace sign but the center fell out, so don't do that. *(Looking at CATHY's work)* Oh, like just a free-formed continuous line. That's great.

CATHY: Thanks. That's enough.

JUDY: No, as long as we're gonna do it. His insurance will pay for it. Just think of no child support payments for six months — and he's taking out his new girlfriend every night — took her to fucking Las Vegas! Restaurants I'll never see the inside of! Buys the kids toys, clothes, whatever shit they want, but no child support for me. He's Santa Claus — I'm the Wicked Witch of the West. Trying to teach values that *nobody believes in any more!!*

CATHY: Let's do the other side.

JUDY: I'm not into it any more.

CATHY: Come on. Watergate. And — and all the lies about everything.

JUDY: All the bullshit.

CATHY: Nixon.

JUDY: Marilyn Monroe and John F. Kennedy doing it. Martin Luther King's sex life.

CATHY: Backing dictators — calling them democrats.

JUDY: Fucking with the destinies of other countries. Pardoning each other for criminal acts!

CATHY: Killing presidents — our own!!

JUDY: Selling us!! Selling us!! *(Stops) Shit!!!* I'm out of propane!

CATHY: So am I.

JUDY: *See??!* Nothing fucking *works!!!*

(They exit.)

(JIM is sitting on the couch, staring at the television. EVELYN enters and watches him.)

VOICEOVER: They watch hours of television.

(EVELYN crosses to JIM and comes up behind him and embraces him around the neck. Then she begins to rub his neck. After a beat or so, she sits next to him on the couch and puts her legs on his lap. During all of this, JIM has continued to look at the TV, but responds unconsciously to EVELYN — he doesn't resist her. She kisses him and he responds, but the TV catches his attention again. EVELYN takes JIM by the hand and leads him off into the bedroom. A count of fifty, EVELYN returns alone. She sits on the couch and stares at the TV.)

JIM: *(Offstage)* Honey? Honey? My leg's gone to sleep. Isn't that funny?

(EVELYN doesn't get up.)

(Sound of cheap top forty from a bar. JERRY and JUDY are sitting separately — a seat or two between them. JUDY checks her watch: She's waiting for someone.)

VOICEOVER: Where genders meet. *(After a beat, JERRY begins to speak — to no one in particular. Trying not to, JUDY notices him out of the corner of her eye. JERRY sees this and then begins to deliver the speech directly to her.)*

JERRY: Lincoln was elected president in 1860. Kennedy was elected president in 1960. Both men were involved in civil rights for Negroes. Both men were assassinated, on a Friday, in the presence of their wives. Each wife had lost a baby, a male child in fact, while they were living at the White House. Both men had a bullet wound that entered the head from behind. Both men were succeeded by vice-presidents named Johnson who were southern democrats and former senators. Both Johnsons were born one hundred years apart — in 1808 and 1908, respectively. Lincoln was killed in Ford's Theatre. Kennedy was killed while riding in a Lincoln convertible made by the Ford Motor Company. John Wilkes Booth and Lee Harvey Oswald were born in 1839 and 1939, respectively, and had the same number of letters in their names. The first name of Lincoln's private secretary was John—the last name of Kennedy's private secretary was Lincoln.

JUDY: *Will you leave me the fuck alone?*

JERRY: Think about it. Life can be understood. You come in here a lot. You like the bartender?

JUDY: I don't like anyone!! I have responsibilities!!! (JUDY *exits.* JERRY *sits for a moment, then squeaks involuntarily and exits.*)

(JUDY *enters, yelling.*)

JUDY: Jason! Jennifer! Jason! Jennifer! *(Sees them, exits—the next several lines are done from offstage.)* Get offa her!! *Jason!!* Right now!! *(Pause)* Don't hit him with that!*(Pause)* Jennifer!! Give me that!! Where did you *get* that?!*(Pause)* Jason!! Leave her alone!! *Jennifer, come back!! Jason—don't run off!!* (To some neighbor) Well, I'm sorry, Lady!! Go live in a fuckin' convent if you don't want to listen to *kids!!* (Back on—to the audience) You haven't seen a skateboard, have you? Picture of Satan with Mick Jagger's tongue—hanging out? No? Orange wheels— *(Exiting)* I live over there—if you see it. Just leave it in that Blue Pinto—none of the doors lock. *(Pause)* Thanks.

VOICEOVER: The de-coding of behavior provides a key to gender identification.

(CATHY *is waiting, looking at her watch.* JUDY *joins her—she's late. They sit for a beat.*)

CATHY: You were so positive!

JUDY: I know.

CATHY: You were so sure.

JUDY: I know.

CATHY: It's incredible!

JUDY: You're telling me. Two Corvettes that much alike! And what the hell did that—that—Cambodian—

CATHY: You said he was from Thailand.

JUDY: Whatever—some skinny oriental guy—anyway, what did he think he was doing parking a car like that on a residential street?

CATHY: He, probably, foolishly, thought it would be safe here.

JUDY: Well, he doesn't know anything—he's just asking questions. What's he doing with a Corvette, anyway?

CATHY: What do we do?

JUDY: Jagger thinks he's got a way into the police computer—if it comes to that.

CATHY: No way!! I'm not encouraging that kid—he's scary enough already.

JUDY: We might be arrested—they know it's two women.

CATHY: They know it's two women! They know it's two women! Oh my god, oh my god, oh my god! How can they know that!?

JUDY: They heard giggling.

CATHY: Giggling! Giggling! Who was giggling? I wasn't giggling. You were giggling!

JUDY: No, I wasn't. I was distraught! I still am!

CATHY: You're distraught! You're distraught! I'm the one who's distraught! Look at my life! It's falling apart!

JUDY: And what do you think mine's doing? Singing a little song?

(A beat)

CATHY: What's his plan? Jagger?

JUDY: Zap the records — it's easy, he says.

CATHY: Good. Good. Tell him we'll pay him in cash.

(JUDY *exits, leaving* CATHY. CATHY *starts to exit, addresses the audience.*)

CATHY: *(To the audience)* Lately, I've been having trouble breathing. Several times a day, I forget how. I'll notice that I'm running out of breath because I haven't exhaled. So I exhale, and then I'm fine until a few hours later and I realize that I'm out of breath again. So I inhale or exhale, whichever is appropriate.

(JERRY *enters.* CATHY *crosses to join him — they are in his house.*)

VOICEOVER: They are concerned with interior decoration.

JERRY: So I'm tearing out that entire wall. Open this all up.

CATHY: Uh-huh.

JERRY: Then I buy good furniture. *(Squeaks)*

CATHY: Uh-huh.

JERRY: I might take out that wall, too.

CATHY: Don't want to take out too many walls.

JERRY: Well, then, no more — just those two. *(Squeaks)*

CATHY: Uh-huh.

JERRY: How's the therapy?

CATHY: What therapy?

JERRY: Right. Right. That's the best kind. In my opinion. *(Emits a high-pitched rhythmic laugh)*

CATHY: *(Starts to leave)* Well, I should —

JERRY: Yes. *(Pause)* Did you enjoy the magazine?

CATHY: It was...interesting. *(Returning the magazine to him)*

JERRY: *(Giving it back to her)* Keep it.

CATHY: I'm having a hard time reading, lately. Everything seems to be some kind of message.

JERRY: Message?! Yes. Did you see my ad? Wait— *(Finds it, shows it to her)* Read it.

CATHY: *(Reads)* "Top-Risk Action Group for hire by individuals, organizations, and governments. Rescue a speciality. Call The Watcher, (719) 555-9564. Before noon or after midnight. *(Pause)* But you're not a group.

JERRY: I can be.

CATHY: I have to go. Thanks for the dinner.

JERRY: Next time I'll get the hot mustard sauce instead of the sweet and sour. And more fries.

CATHY: Thanks.

JERRY: And a hot apple pie for you. If you want it.

CATHY: Thanks.

JERRY: I wouldn't want to get it if you didn't want it.

CATHY: Thanks.

JERRY: *(Squeaks)* Bye.

CATHY: Bye.

(She exits. JERRY bangs his head against something, exits.)

(In another space, CATHY re-enters, reads from the magazine.)

CATHY: The young Basque terrorist, age 16, walked
Out of the apartment house
On Calle Reina Cristina Street
Heading toward his car.
He froze in mid-stride,

Slapped a hand to the side of his head,
As if he had just remembered something very
important,
And fell to the asphalt, dead.

The bullet that killed him
Was fired by a friend,
A fellow terrorist from another faction,
Hiding in the lobby of the apartment building
They shared.

Who are the Basques?

(ERIC *enters, dressed in a couple layers of clothing—he
carries a pair of sweatpants which he puts on over his two
pair of pants, and a full knapsack.* CATHY *enters with an
empty suitcase.*)

CATHY: What is this? I found this in your room.
What are you doing?

ERIC: Getting dressed.

CATHY: Have you gone *crazy???* You're putting on
layers of clothing!!!

ERIC: Bag is too small. Cheap piece of shit—not even
Samsonite—embarrassing.

CATHY: Eric, what...is...this.

ERIC: I'm outta here.

CATHY: You are *not!!!*

ERIC: Yep.

CATHY: *(Grabbing him)* You are *not!!! Not, not!!!* Take *offf*
these clothes!!! *Now!!!* Take them *off* take them *off, take
them offffff!!!!!*

ERIC: Mom, please. I'm much stronger than you. Just let
me go. *(She holds on. He looks at her, then firmly, but
gently, removes her arms from his body.)* I sold my stereo.
Girl I met's taking me to the airport. I'll be at Dad's.

This is his number— *(Hands her a scrap of paper)* —just in
case you burned it or something. *(Picks up knapsack. He
then places his open hand on top of his mother's head in an
awkward gesture of affection.)* Bye. Say "bye" to Grandma
and—him—for me. (ERIC *waddles off—his bulk making
him look like a toddler.* CATHY *sits on the floor for a beat,
then gets up slowly. Horn honk—she runs to say
goodbye—we see her wave, but weakly, because he's already
gone and doesn't see her.)*

(JIM *wanders through.)*

JIM: There's nothing wrong with me.

CATHY: *Then it must be us!!! Huh???? We* must be *fucked
up!!!* Because it can't be *you!!! Noooooo!! (Beat)* Oh, Dad.
(She embraces him and breaks down.)

JIM: Oh, Honey— Shhhhhh. Shhhhhh. Shhhhhhh.
(Wipes away her tears) Who was that fat kid that just
went out the door? He go to your school? *(Resigned,*
CATHY *exits.)*

JIM: Now where was I? Oh— *(Points, offstage)* There.
(He exits.)

(CATHY *exits.* JUDY *enters and sings.)*

JUDY: *(Singing)* O crocodile night,
You've always been there,
In the thin air,
Or on the dune.
O crocodile night,
You're always waiting,
Tonight you're mating
With the moon. *(Pause)*
The song of the hamper,
The song of the screen,
The song of the dishes,
The song of the green,
The song of the streetlights,

The song of the park,
The song of the lawnchair,
The song of the dark. *(To her offstage children, at the top of
her lungs) Now for Chrissake go to sleep! (She exits.)*

VOICEOVER: Why they sing is under investigation.

*(*JERRY *is sleeping — suddenly he is surrounded by* ALIENS.
They lift him up, carry him away — he wakes up during this.)

JERRY: *Aaaaaaaaaaeeeeeeeeeeeee!*

*(*ALIENS *exit with* JERRY.*)*

VOICEOVER: This is a good place for an intermission.

END OF ACT ONE

ACT TWO

(To signal the end of the intermission, JIM *enters and begins talking to the audience. He is in possession of all his faculties. After a few beats of the speech,* CATHY *enters, drawn by this vision of* JIM, *and listens.)*

JIM: Jack's a smart guy, smarter than me in a lot of ways. I'm a carpenter by trade and, before the war, I did my apprenticeship on stick-built, lath-and-plaster houses. One-inch boards laid diagonally on studs with sixteen-inch centers. Hell — pounds of nails. Tens of thousands of nails for one house. Then I got drafted and when I came home, we started putting up roof trusses and making walls of three-quarters or five-eights inch sheet rock. You know there's no rock in sheet rock — it's just plaster pressed between two sheets of heavy paper. That's what's in my home.

CATHY: I dreamed about Dad the way he used to be.

JIM: Jack's getting into modular homes which you buy pre-fab in two to four sections which you haul to the site and put together. Now these have one-eighth inch paneling made of wood products that have been fused into a solid sheet and melded with a surface of plastic photo-reproduction of your favorite wood-grain. These houses go up very fast, of course, and sometimes come with the curtains already on the windows. People laugh, but why today would you want to build a house that would last a hundred years? Think of the changes in the last hundred years. Can you imagine the next hundred? What will be here—right where I'm standing? All the nails in the world won't keep those walls from cracking when the bulldozer comes. So Jack is right. I mean that. (JIM *exits*. EVELYN *enters*.)

EVELYN: I figured it out. We're going to get in the car. And we're going to travel west.

CATHY: What good will that do?

EVELYN: It's worked for our families for 200 years. We started in New Jersey and Massachusetts. We've managed a state about every two generations.

CATHY: But we're already in the west.

EVELYN: There's more to go.

CATHY: I don't understand how this will help.

EVELYN: I don't believe in medical science. They're making it up as they go along. They laugh at us when we leave the room.

CATHY: Will Dad go?

EVELYN: When I put him in the car. I'll just pack him up. As soon as we start to drive, his brain will start to clear. Memories will come flooding in. Vocabulary, too. Words of songs he's forgotten. Jokes. Anecdotes. Our life together—it's all floating around in the air. We just have to gather, gather it in. I'm gonna keep driving until he's back together. It may take as far as San Diego, but I'm not stopping until every piece is there again.

CATHY: What about Eric?

EVELYN: We'll put a message on the answering machine.

CATHY: We don't have an answering machine.

EVELYN: We'll *get one!!*

(*They exit.*)

(ERIC *crosses to a pay phone, puts in a dime, dials, gets the* ANSWERING MACHINE MESSAGE.) *[The following voices are on the answering machine.]*

CATHY's VOICE: Hello. Eric? This is Mom. We've taken a little trip.

EVELYN's VOICE: For your Grandpa—to make him better.

JIM's VOICE: Huh? What is this thing?

CATHY's VOICE: Please come home anyway—a neighbor will let you in. Please.

VOICE OF TELEPHONE OPERATOR: Please deposit fifty cents for an additional minute—please— (ERIC *can't get his money fast enough—he gets a dial tone—he beats the phone with the receiver, hangs it up, exits.)*

(EVELYN *and* CATHY *are in the car, traveling.* JIM *is lying down in the back seat.)*

EVELYN: Do you have any idea where we are?

CATHY: Where else? The car.

EVELYN: Jim?

CATHY: Mom, we've been traveling in circles—I don't know where the hell we are.

(EVELYN *looks in the back seat.)*

EVELYN: Jim—?

CATHY: On the plains somewhere. Mom? What is it?

EVELYN: We'd better go back.

CATHY: Is he all right?

EVELYN: Please. It didn't work.

(JIM *sits up, looks out window.)*

JIM: There's that old man again. That spindly-legged old guy running against the side of the car.

EVELYN: What?

JIM: Been running alongside me all my life. Look at him go.

EVELYN: *(To* CATHY*)* He's talking!

CATHY: What're you talking about, Dad?

JIM: That old guy — that long-legged old man. Boy, can he run.

EVELYN: It's working.

CATHY: What old man?

JIM: Look.

CATHY: Oh, him.

EVELYN: Where? Where?

CATHY: Rows of something, Mom. It's rows of corn or something out the window. See?

JIM: Running, running, running. Oh, it's a strange place — this...where are we?

(EVELYN and CATHY look quickly at each other, panicked — decide to lie.)

EVELYN: Idaho.

CATHY: *(Overlapping* EVELYN*)* Nevada.

EVELYN: Nevada.

CATHY: *(Overlapping* EVELYN*)* Arizona.

JIM: Are we lost?

CATHY & EVELYN: *(Together)* No.

JIM: *(Heavy hillbilly)* Hey, hey, HEY! Your boy pissed in the snow outside my cabin. It's frozen there! *(Another hillbilly voice)* It'll thaw next spring — what's your worry? *(First hillbilly voice)* I recognize my daughter's handwriting! *(Another memory comes)* Uh — uh — uh —

This is the forest Primeval, the murmuring pines and
hemlock, bearded in moss and in garments green, stand
like Druids of eld with beards that rest on
their — their — *(Trying not to let his memory loss stop
him — he sings:)* Sometimes I wonder why I spend these
lonely hours, dreaming of a song,
a melody...haunts my...memory....*(Speaks)* Stop the car.
(Gets out of car) Left — loose. Right — tight. Left loose.
Right tight. Crying so loud — must be a boy. No, it's a
little girl — it's a little, little girl — (EVELYN *gets out of the
car —* JIM *grabs her and takes her to him, as if to dance.)*
Evelyn — we're making love in the graveyard and
scaring the hell out of those kids. They think our
sounds are coming from the dead lying below us.
(Scared, breaks from her) My tongue's stuck on the
clothesline! Trying to lick the ice — Mama, Mama, help!
(Really reverting) First bath outside in sun.
Fireflies in jar.
Night-night. *(Climbs back in the car)*
Warm pee.
Bosom.
Mmmmm. Mmmmm. Mmmmmm.
Shhhhhhh. *(He lies back down.)*

EVELYN: *(After a long beat)* Jim?

CATHY: What happened?

EVELYN: *(Gets back in the car, upset)* He was dreaming.
I guess. Let's go home.

(CATHY breathes a sigh of relief. EVELYN *glares at her.)*

CATHY: I'm sorry — I'm just so worried about Eric.

EVELYN: *(Pretending to forget with a vengeance who her
grandson is)* Who?

CATHY: Mom!

EVELYN: Sorry.

CATHY: Which way?

EVELYN: I don't know!

CATHY: Tell me which way!

EVELYN: For Chrissakes! You're a grown up!! *Pick one!!*

CATHY: We'll go this way.

EVELYN: What are you *doing?* It's that way!!

VOICEOVER: They often dream they have been abducted by extraterrestrials.

(ALIEN *played by the* JUDY *actor is reading a copy of the "National Enquirer" — she notices the picture of an alien on the front of it, looks at it closely, then puts it into a large Zip-loc bag and seals it. Other* ALIENS *enter, rolling* JERRY *in on a dolly — he wakes up and opens his mouth to scream, but can't make a sound.)*

ALIEN: *(Putting her face very close to* JERRY's *face and talking very deliberately)*
What — can — we — do — about — your — fear?

(JERRY *can't answer — he just stares at them, screaming silently. They massage his jaws and shut his mouth for him. They all begin to pet him roughly to comfort him, like inept children stroking a dog. They proceed with an examination — it should satirize the examination of field scientists on* "National Geographic" *of an animal in the wild. They measure him, take blood, etc., — all with the air of completely dispassionate scientists. One* ALIEN *finds a pair of clip-on sunglasses in* JERRY's *pocket, holds them up for other* ALIENS *to see, and they all laugh rhythmically. An* ALIEN *produces* Playboy *magazine, opens it to the centerfold, and moves it in front of* JERRY, *trying to arouse him. Another* ALIEN *unzips* JERRY's *fly, looks inside, and waits for an erection. After a beat,* ALIEN *takes out a Dustbuster and inserts it into* JERRY's *pants through his fly and turns it on briefly.*

JERRY *reacts as the semen is sucked from him. This finishes
the exam. An* ALIEN *tags* JERRY *on his ear, zaps him
unconscious, and they lay him down gently and exit.)*

*(*EVELYN *and* CATHY *are looking at snapshots of their trip
west.)*

EVELYN: Here we are at the Blasted Pine. *(Pause)*
Here's that rock that looks like a —

CATHY: —baked potato.

EVELYN: Yes. *(Pause)* Here we are at Glen Canyon.

CATHY: Full of water.

EVELYN: They filled it in. *(She passes through several
pictures quickly.)* That's the rest of Utah. He wouldn't let
me stop the car, so these are all blurry.

CATHY: He seemed to be in such a hurry.

EVELYN: No, he still knows he hates —

CATHY: —the Mormons. Yeah.

EVELYN: Here's —

CATHY: —Reno.

EVELYN: *(Correcting her)* Las Vegas. *(Pause)* Here's —

CATHY: Death Valley.

EVELYN: *(Correcting her)* Barstow. *(Pause)* Here's San
Bernadino. *(Pause)* Here we are at...at the zoo.

CATHY: Where?

EVELYN: San Diego.

CATHY: Who's this guy with the wet drawers, walking
out of the picture? He's looking off to the right, like he
doesn't notice...he looks so...old...he's lost, completely
lost. *(She exits.)*

EVELYN: Here's the other Blasted Pine. *(Pause)* Here's
the Pacific Ocean. *(Pause)* Here's a shell on the beach.

(Pause) Here's a piece of a shell. *(Pause)* Here's a sliver of driftwood. *(Pause)* Here's....*(She exits with the snapshots.)*

VOICEOVER: They seem to enjoy what is called dreaming—

(During the VOICEOVER, CATHY *joins* JUDY *outside—they are smoking dope.)*

VOICEOVER: —and spend one-third of their lives in this comatose state, allowing their minds to make stories of whatever stimuli are left over from the day or the life. Significance is then divined from these neural and electronic collages and the process is deemed therapeutic.

JUDY: I found this in Jason's drawer.

CATHY: What? No—all of a sudden I feel so weird smoking this now.

JUDY: I grounded him for life.

CATHY: That's a long time when you're his age. This *is* good.

JUDY: Imagine what it does to the brain of a twelve-year-old?

CATHY: So, anyway, you were Eve? Man.

JUDY: I can't control my subconscious, alright? Would you rather hear the Spider Dream?

CATHY: No!

JUDY: Okay. I was naked in the Garden and I was looking at all the leaves and stuff and, suddenly, it really began to grow right before my eyes—you know, like that speeded-up photography on nature programs of the opening of a flower or whatever? But this was closing up—you know—the leaves out of control, covering up the sky.

CATHY: Like kudzu.

JUDY: Yeah. Like some paradisical kudzu—some mojo kudzu—

CATHY: —of Eternity.

JUDY: No, not Eternity—don't say that.

CATHY: Okeedokee.

JUDY: And the fruit got real big and started hanging lower and lower on the trees. Ever seen a cow that needs to be milked and the farmer's on vacation or something? Mooo. Moooo. Ridiculous, man. I mean, moooooooo. I'm a cow.

CATHY: You're not a cow.

JUDY: I don't want to be a cow.

CATHY: You don't have to be a cow.

JUDY: What is this? Some feminist accusatory bullshit? I know I don't have to be a cow.

CATHY: Listen—are you listening? What was I talking about? I mean, it's not belief. It's feeling. You feel things. And maybe they are assholes. But it's love. How can love be bad? I mean, love is good.

JUDY: Love is very good.

CATHY: Yes, we love and that's good.

JUDY: But we're fucked.

CATHY: Oh, yeah. Go on, I am listening.

JUDY: At that very moment—

CATHY: What moment?

JUDY: In this Garden. Keep up.

CATHY: The Snake.

JUDY: No. No Snake. The Snake was in the next grove, helping Adam—

CATHY: Helping Adam name things.

JUDY: At that very moment—

CATHY: Like the Blue-Footed Booby.

JUDY: I hear this something—sound. Sssssssss.

CATHY: It is a snake!

JUDY: No snake. Get off of this snake thing!

CATHY: Then what was it?

JUDY: Pressure.

CATHY: God.

JUDY: No. The Tree. The Major Tree. The whole place.

CATHY: What? This is the Knowledge?

JUDY: Yeah. It was all about to bust—*open!* So I just sort of jumped—like Superman? And it worked! So— whoosh—I flew up through the limbs, through the Mojo Paradisical Kudzu, and—whoosh—broke through all the Green stuff. *(Pause)* And I was *free!* And the light poured in—

CATHY: And then you woke up.

JUDY: What?

CATHY: You woke up. You were dreaming all this.

JUDY: Oh yeah. I woke up—I woke up.

CATHY: Alone.

JUDY: No—he was there. The guy—you know.

CATHY: You lucky...

JUDY: I'd been flying. I had felt so free. And I looked down and what did I have in my hand? The Fruit of the

Tree — still sticky, the little bishop, its one eye staring blankly at me.

CATHY: Oh, that fruit, the passion fruit, the forbidden fruit, the fruit of forgetfulness.

JUDY: *(Long pause)* I finally told him I loved him — love him. You know, just sitting there — not in the throes of passion or anything.

CATHY: Not again.

JUDY: Different guy — they don't know each other.

CATHY: What did this one say?

JUDY: "We don't have time for abstractions." And then he said, "Be here now."

CATHY: So that was it.

JUDY: Oh no, I'm seeing him next Sunday. I love him. Really. Everything's gonna be fine.

CATHY: Wake up, Jude.

JUDY: Well, at least I'm trying. You're not even *trying*. At least I'm trying to be *alive*.

(JUDY exits. EVELYN enters.)

EVELYN: I'm leaving for the ah —

CATHY: Oh, Mom! Judy just left — I — Should I go?

EVELYN: No, it's my day. Thursday. Thursday is my day.

CATHY: I took him the —

EVELYN: Good. Did he ah — ?

CATHY: Yeah. Well, a little. His eyes seemed to...a little.

EVELYN: Oh, well, then he must've known —

CATHY: Oh, he knew. He — Sure.

EVELYN: Well, I've got some new — *(Holds up one of those plastic bags from a mall store)*

CATHY: Great.

EVELYN: So — *(She exits.)*

CATHY: Tell him — *(She waves instead.)*

CATHY: *(To herself)* Get straight. Get straight. Wake *up!*

(JERRY wakes up. CATHY doesn't notice and exits.)

JERRY: Hmmmmmmmmm. *(Stretches)* Oh my God, I'm outside!!! Oh my God, I'm lying *in my driveway! (Looks around to see if the neighbors see him—checks his watch.)* Oh my God, I've got to get to work! Oh my God, my fly is open! Oh my God, I hope I'm an alcoholic! *(He exits.)*

(CATHY is on the phone.)

CATHY: Finally.
Yes. May I speak to Eric, please.
Well, then, let me speak to his—his father.
Yes, "Michael." *(Waits)* Hello, Mike?
Where's Eric—is he there or over at Todd's?
You *what?????*
Well, he's not!! He's *not* here!!!! When did he leave?
A week ago!!! A week ago!!! We've been gone for a week and a half!!!!
You put him on the *plane* and *never called me?????*
OhmyGod ohmyGod ohmyGod ohmyGod. *Didn't* you *worry* when you didn't *hear from him???*
I know he doesn't call *a lot!!* Well, *ever*—alright—*but why didn't you call me to see if he arrived!!!!*
Hello?? Hello!!
This is *who????*
Nice to *meet me??? Where is my son!!!!*
What do *mean* "He can take care of himself!!" How do *you* know? You're only 18 yourself!!! *Go practice your fucking oboe!!!*
Mike? *Mike!!* What are you doing!!! Our *son* is lost

somewhere between New York and Colorado and you put your *child girlfriend* on the *phone????*
"*Only* the Midwest?" What do you think the Midwest is — Rhode Island? *Look at a map, you imbecile!!!* It's *huge!!!*
No, I will *not* calm down. *You will* call the airline and check the passenger list and find out if he had to change planes. And if he did, *where* — and *pray* he didn't land at *O'Hare* — that's in Chicago, by the way.
I'll wait up for your report!! *(Hangs up)* Mom? *Mom! Mooooooooooommmmmmmmmmm!!!!! (She crosses, looking for* EVELYN, *runs into* JERRY.)

JERRY: I'm looking for my sunglasses.

CATHY: *(Turning and crossing away from him)* Mooommmmmm!

JERRY: Are you looking for your mother now? (CATHY *exits.)* And sometimes therapy just makes things worse. I know. I understand. *(He speaks to the audience.)* I talk to her so much better when she's not here. *(He exits.)*

(JIM *and* EVELYN *are looking at menus.)*

JIM: I'm gonna get the country chicken. I know that's boring, 'cause I always get it.

EVELYN: Wait — how did we get here? Oh my god — something...

JIM: No — sometimes I get the liver and onions. That's good. Their liver and onions is good.

EVELYN: Jim — where's the desk? Where's the...nurse? I was holding a straw for you, I —

JIM: They have *some* good things here.

EVELYN: You're so much better all of a sudden.

JIM: You know you're at Big Boy. The table is sticky.

EVELYN: *(Feeling the table)* It is! It is! Oh, it *is!!*

JIM: Look at those plants.

EVELYN: Are they — ?

JIM: Real. They're real. Those are real plants.

EVELYN: It's beautiful in here. The Big Boy is beautiful.

JIM: How do they water all these plants? They probably stand on the booths. *(Beat)* I'm gonna get the salad bar.

EVELYN: Me, too.

JIM: *(About the plants)* Maybe that *is* the salad bar. (EVELYN *is staring across from them at something, doesn't respond.)* Do you think? Baby?

EVELYN: Look at that couple over there.

JIM: What.

EVELYN: Over there.

JIM: She looks sort of like you.

EVELYN: No, *him.* He reminds me of you — kind of.

JIM: Am I that skinny?

EVELYN: He's not skinny.

JIM: He's skinny.

EVELYN: And she looks like —

JIM: Oh no, you're much prettier than that, Baby.

EVELYN: Don't look!

JIM: Did she see us? It doesn't matter. She's probably thinking the same thing we are.

EVELYN: Oh my God — Don't look.

JIM: Damn! I'm missing something good. What's wrong?

EVELYN: I don't know.

JIM: What's *he* doing?

EVELYN: He's just sitting there, staring.

JIM: Are they having a fight?

EVELYN: No. She's holding a straw for him — ohmyGod.

JIM: What?

EVELYN: Wait. *(She moves her hand up very slowly and moves it back and forth, watching the woman while she does it, as if she is checking her reflection in a mirror.)*

JIM: What are you doing, Evelyn?

EVELYN: Shhhhh. *(She moves her body back and forth, watching the woman, then does one quick hand movement, turns away, thinks, looks back at woman — stops, stares, bewildered and afraid.)*

JIM: I can't take you anywhere.

EVELYN: *(Grabbing JIM's hand)* Let's get out of here.

JIM: I don't care. I'm looking. *(Looks at woman, looks away)* She's crying and looking at us. What's wrong?

EVELYN: She's remembering — she's remembering —

JIM: *What?*

EVELYN: She's remembering *now.* Oh *God*, let's get *out* of here!

JIM: Evelyn, Baby — *(EVELYN drags JIM by the hand.)*

EVELYN: Come on — while we've still got some *time!!!*

(She exits, pulling him — he laughs, following her, still not understanding.)

(Female ALIEN enters and gives this report in a smooth documentary style. It is juxtaposed with the actions of JERRY, who is fantasizing about CATHY.)

ALIEN: Hello. This segment of our presentation is about masochism.

(During the following speech, JERRY sits and imagines CATHY. He begins to become aroused. His FANTASY CATHY

*swoops in and kisses him passionately — she swoops away and
he still can feel her there. He continues to imagine
love-making, laughter, and himself being witty. The fantasy
is broken, when the real* CATHY *enters after the masochism
speech is over. Then* JERRY *returns to his state of nervousness
and fear with her.)*

ALIEN: Masochism is a rather disorganized but,
nevertheless, growing religion with many followers of
both genders. It seems to be a form of worship of the
Mating Process by celibate nonparticipants and centers
on, usually, the idealization of the Worship-Object.
The ceremonies are held in private and usually include
solitary fertility rites. Prayer is also solitary and silent
and can be observed several times a day, depending on
the devotion of the Masochistic supplicant. *(*FANTASY
CATHY *enters.)* *(Pause)* The Object is called up through
telepathy, conversations and encounters are
constructed by the supplicant, and the mating act is
imagined silently. The experienced Masochist can pray
at any time, anywhere. Once the Worship-Object has
been selected and a true masochistic state has been
achieved, the Masochist eschews contact with the real
Object— *(*FANTASY CATHY *exits.)* —communicating
only when necessary, and then through broken
sentences or a high-pitched rhythmic laughter.
This action is designed to repel the real Object, thereby
protecting the contemplative life of the now securely
celibate Masochist.

(The ALIEN *presenter has exited and the real* CATHY *enters,
sees* JERRY.*)*

CATHY: Hello.

*(*JERRY *emits a high-pitched, rhythmic laugh.)*

CATHY: *(Starting to exit)* See you.

JERRY: Excuse—

CATHY: *(Not seeing him)* Huh?

JERRY: I've avoiding you—been— Me—sorry.

CATHY: I just came to talk.

JERRY: Thank—thank you. A lot on mind—my mind. Things...happen...to...me. *(He exits, laughing with his high-pitched, nervous laugh.)*

CATHY: Me, too. You're not the only one things happen to! You know?! I'd like to be weird! I'd love to have permission to be weird! *(She exits.)*

VOICEOVER: They wash their clothes in public places.

(JERRY and EVELYN are in a laundromat—they've never met, but JERRY begins talking.)

JERRY: Black eggs, warm rocks, gelatinous material falling from the sky—I mean, were these people all crazy? Think of the toads! Great storms of toads, falling in deluges, piling up on the roads. Fish! In Singapore, it rained fish. And Ed Mootz of Cincinnati and his peach tree destroyed by red glop that fell from some strange-looking cloud—there's a picture of him standing by his dead tree in a book I have at home. Angel hair and star jelly— scientists always laugh at these—but people have picked this stuff up. I'm not kidding! Not to mention the weird metal shit that falls from the sky and the ice—brains some old lady or destroys her television. And you hand 'em the goddam thing and they put it in one of those giant baggies and take it away. And that's the last you ever hear of it! *(Long beat as EVELYN looks at him)*

EVELYN: People—people on game shows buying vowels because they don't know the most commonest phrase. I mean—ignorance.

JERRY: *(After a beat)* Baron Rodemire de Tarazone of France was assassinated by Claude Volbonne—

twenty-one years earlier, Baron Rodemire de Tarazone's father had been assassinated and by a man named Claude Volbonne. But it was a different Claude Volbonne and they were not related!!!

EVELYN: And that second dryer is *shot!*

JERRY: I know — I lost a quarter in it last week.

EVELYN: They say they're working on these things. They say, "We're working on it!" "Lady!" But are they? I mean, where are the results?! And for that matter, where are they? Huh? When was the last time you actually saw someone in charge? I mean, in the flesh?

JERRY: On television.

EVELYN: Exactly! On television.

JERRY: On television.

EVELYN: When was the last time you saw the person who owns this laundromat? I mean, *who is in charge? Who is running this place? Huh?!*

JERRY: *(Grabbing* EVELYN*)* That's what I want to know!

EVELYN: That's what I want to know, too!

JERRY: I really want to know that.

EVELYN: So do I.

JERRY: *(Letting go of her)* Excuse me.

EVELYN: *(Quickly folding a piece of her laundry)* I usually do this at home.

JERRY: Not me. I do it in public all the time. I think it's job stress.

EVELYN: My dryer's broken.

JERRY: *(About the incompetency of the world)* Of course. Is someone working on it?

EVELYN: My husband's boss. I mean, his ex-boss, came over and tried, but...

JERRY: An *ex*-boss, of course. Power just...leaks.

EVELYN: *(Thinking about JIM and everything)* How can a country that sent a man to the moon—

JERRY: Maybe they didn't. Maybe he didn't go.

EVELYN: You mean he didn't go?

JERRY: Maybe.

EVELYN: But we saw it.

JERRY: Where?

EVELYN: *(She gets it.)* On television! *(Pause)* How did I used to know things? I mean, when we first came here, it was just a bunch of houses built on concrete slabs. The contractor's wife named all the streets. My husband helped build it. And now you're telling me it was all a dream?

JERRY: No—no, we're awake! I know that.

EVELYN: I can't sleep.

JERRY: *(Coming to her, very tender)* You need to sleep. You should sleep.

EVELYN: I'm afraid to close my eyes. Change happens so fast. *(JERRY and EVELYN sit silently next to each other, watching the clothes turn in the dryer.)*

VOICEOVER: Change happens.

(Sound of country music—EVELYN arises from her chair in the laundromat, leaving her laundry. She crosses and exits with purpose. JERRY picks up her laundry and tries to pursue her.)

JERRY: Wait. Wait!! Wait!! Come back!! *(To audience)* Why do people always say that? Like—someone steals your car and you yell, "Hey, come back here!" like they're going to put on the brakes, back-up, and give you back your car. I mean, if they wanted to come back, they would.

(EVELYN *has re-entered and is lying on the floor of a shower in her panties. She is curled into a tight knot. Sound of a shower dripping. She's asleep. Upstage is a bed with a large lump in it and a chair with a pile of clothes by it.*)

EVELYN: (*A drip from the shower hits her.*) What? (*Half wakes up, shivers, reaches for something like someone who's thrown off the covers, finds a shirt, puts it on, sits up, looks up at the shower.*) I'm in a shower.

VOICEOVER: She is in a shower.

(EVELYN *stands, burps, waits, burps, crosses to a chair, sits. She finds a man's boots and puts them on. She finds cigarettes and lights up.*)

EVELYN: These aren't my boots.

VOICEOVER: Motel. Mo — tel. When a traveler is tired, a motel is used.

(EVELYN *crosses to curtain, shuffling in the boots, parts the curtain, reads a neon sign.*)

EVELYN: Ang-La. Ang-La. Ang-La. Angri— Shangri—

VOICEOVER: She doesn't know where she is.

EVELYN: Shangri-La. Oh.

(*A large mound of blankets sits up and speaks.*)

JACK: Baby? Where are ya?

EVELYN: Who is that?

JACK: (*The mound lays back down.*) Jack. Jack. Hey, I'm a little queasy — okay, baby?

(EVELYN *starts to gather her stuff, frantically.*)

EVELYN: What am I doing? What am I doing? Oh my God. That's it—I'm alone. *(She looks off in space for a beat while her aloneness hits her, then exits in* JACK's *shirt and boots.)*

JACK: Evelyn? Evelyn? It wasn't charity. *(Beat. No answer.)* I knew it. Damn.

*(*CATHY *is sitting in the house, surrounded by maps — the TV is on.* JERRY *enters with* EVELYN's *laundry — he puts it down beside* CATHY. CATHY *looks at him and he exits. After a beat,* CATHY *hears someone else entering the house from the opposite direction.)*

CATHY: Mom?

EVELYN: *(Offstage)* Yeah?

CATHY: Where you been?

EVELYN: *(Still offstage)* Oh—out with some friends. I ran into some people I knew at the—the—they asked about your dad, so I—I....

VOICEOVER: Never force anything.

CATHY: Anybody I know? *(*EVELYN *enters, her coat on and wearing* JACK's *boots, carrying a grocery bag.)*

EVELYN: No. Heard anything from Eric?

CATHY: No.

EVELYN: *(Sits on the couch)* Did Mike check on the planes?

CATHY: Yeah. He never got on. He cashed in the ticket. He's a missing person, Mom. *(Rattling the maps)* Look at this! Look at this! This is America. How did it get to be so enormous?

EVELYN: *(Simple statement of fact)* We took it from the Indians.

CATHY: That's not Eric's fault! I mean, what are we supposed to do with all this land?! Didn't anybody think about that?!! I mean, didn't anybody think back then that people could get *lost?!!* Didn't anybody think about the *Goddamn future?!*

EVELYN: What's an A P B?

CATHY: I tried to get one. He's not a criminal. I'm gonna go to bed — I'm gonna sleep with this telephone.

EVELYN: Stranger things have happened.

CATHY: What's in the bag?

EVELYN: Clothes.

CATHY: Should I leave the TV on?

EVELYN: Uh-huh.

CATHY: Nice boots.

EVELYN: Thanks.

(CATHY *exits with the telephone.* EVELYN *lies down on the couch, her head on the grocery bag, and stares at the TV. After a beat,* CATHY *re-enters and looks at her mother with curiosity.* EVELYN *doesn't notice her. Unable to figure out what it is exactly that bothers her about* EVELYN, CATHY *quietly exits again.* EVELYN *flicks through the channels with the remote and finds* The Tonight Show *theme.)*

EVELYN: Heeeeeere's Johnny.

(ERIC *is asleep in a mall at night. Suddenly, a Muzak version of* "Raindrops Keep Falling on My Head" *comes over the PA.)*

VOICE ON PA: Hey, Haircut.

ERIC: *(Waking up with a start)* Where — where — where?!!

VOICE ON PA: Up here. The eye.

ERIC: *(To the source of the* VOICE*)* Listen—they told me this was a DEAD mall. They specifically said this was a *dead* mall.

VOICE ON PA: "They"?

ERIC: Nobody.

VOICE ON PA: *(Knowing that* ERIC *is witholding names)* Yeah. Right.

ERIC: I'm outta here. *(Starts to go)*

VOICE ON PA: Says who?

ERIC: I didn't touch nothin'. I didn't do nothin".

VOICE ON PA: Yeah yeah. Listen, Wonder Bread. Get out of here—alright. But you tell the other "Nobodies" to stay away from here, too. And to stop sleeping in the Goodwill Box.

*(*ERIC *tries to get himself to leave—the reality of being outside alone hits him.)*

ERIC: *(To the source of the* VOICE*)* Well, boy, I'm goin'. I'm outta here. *Dude.* I'm hittin' the road. I'm hittin' the fuckin' road, man. I am *out o' here. (He begins to cry.)* Mr. Eye? I'm lost. *(Static on* PA. ERIC *exits.)*

*(*CATHY *is standing, feeding* JIM *in the cafeteria of a nursing home. He is standing, doing a kind of frenetic bounce, like someone whose shoes are stuck to the floor would do to get free. He is staring at a door that sunlight is leaking through. He's lost a great deal of weight—we can see this because his pants are much too big for him. The shirt he's wearing isn't his own—the sleeves are a little too short. And his hair has been slicked back—the effort of a nurse's aide to make the patient look tidy.)*

VOICEOVER: We used to be nomads.

CATHY: *(About the spoon she's holding up to his face)* Here, Dad. Over here. Over here, Dad. Look, Dad. Please.

Please, Dad. Eat. Eat something. Dad — *(He takes a bite and goes back to looking at the door and dancing.)* Good! Want some more? Here's some more. Dad? Dad? Dad? Daddy? *(She holds the spoon out for a couple more beats, then lowers it to the plate.)* They'll put you on an IV, Dad. In your arm. *(She takes his arm and tries to show him.)* They'll put an IV in your arm. Here. If you don't eat. Do you hear me? So you gotta eat — (JIM *is staring at the door.)* What's out there? It's just an old alley. It's just an old dirty alley, filled with garbage cans. And falling down fences. And oil spots. And junk. Stay here and eat. Please. (JIM *crosses to the door in a kind of scooting walk.)* No, Dad! Stay away from the door!

*(*JERRY *enters.)*

JERRY: Don't worry. You have to hold something down and then pull — he won't be able to figure it out. *(About the tray)* Is he done? Well, I gotta take it anyway. *(Takes tray — shouts to* JIM*)* Jim! There's nothing out there! What do you want to go out there for? Here's your daughter to feed you!

CATHY: *(To* JERRY*)* I didn't know you worked here.

JERRY: I told you I'm a nurse.

CATHY: *(To* JERRY*)* Why are you so calm?

JERRY: Am I? Don't worry about the door. He'll get tired of trying. Then we'll put him to bed. *(He exits with tray.)*

CATHY: *(Afterthought, to* JERRY*)* Wait! My father's a mechanical genius! He can figure out how anything works. You don't understand! Hey!

(CATHY *gives up, looks at* JIM. *He's trying the door with no success. She sits and watches him as he continues to try the latch. The lights change to night, and* JIM *slides slowly down the door, exhausted, still holding on to the door handle.)*

VOICEOVER: Light change. Night.

(JERRY *re-enters.*)

JERRY: My shift's done. I thought I'd help put him to bed. *(Crosses to* JIM *and helps him up, removing his hand from the door handle)* Jim? Hey, you're my buddy. *(Getting him up)* That's a boy. *(Straightening out his trousers)* What you want to go out there for anyway? That big, bad world — whew, listen to the news. *(Winking at* CATHY) It's better in here. *(Presenting* JIM) Say goodnight to your daughter. *(*JIM *looks over* CATHY's *head — he doesn't seem to see her.)* He says "Good night." *(*JERRY *exits with him.* CATHY *crosses to the door that* JIM *was struggling with. She opens it with ease and exits.)*

*(*CATHY *sits in the chair in* JERRY's *house.* JERRY *is there and they are listening to Mozart.)*

JERRY: This music came with the house. But I would've bought some, anyway. It's nice to have you here.

CATHY: I've been here lots of times.

JERRY: You never sat down.

CATHY: Oh yeah. *(Beat)* How can you work there?

JERRY: I like to help people. I like to comfort people.

CATHY: I could use...that.

JERRY: Well, the world is round. And we're all on it together. Take off your blouse.

*(*CATHY *unbuttons and tak[es]* ·blouse. JERRY *crosses to her, amazed.)*

JERRY: You're so.... How car.... [t]e in the world with this skin? Look at this beauti....

CATHY: I'm cold. I'm cold. *(*JER.... [embr]aces her.)* This is beautiful music.

JERRY: It's Mozart.

CATHY: He understood, didn't he? He *knew.*

JERRY: Yes, he did. He saw everything—

CATHY: —so clearly. It's like his heart—

JERRY: His *eyes* were open to—

CATHY: —understanding—

JERRY: —that he was being poisoned. He was being poisined and he *knew* it.

CATHY: What?

JERRY: Mozart was being poisoned... what?

CATHY: *(Putting on her blouse)* I—I have to go.

JERRY: Why?

CATHY: This isn't what I meant. You don't understand.

JERRY: But I thought you finally understood. I thought that's why you were here.

CATHY: No, no—it was something about—about just trying to be alive. *(She is exiting.)*

JERRY: But John F. Kennedy, Marilyn Monroe, Martin Luther King—someone murdered them, too. (CATHY *has gone.* JERRY *stops, looks at the audience.)*

JERRY: *(Lost, wanting an answer)* It's not funny, is it? *(To himself, exiting)* Think about it. Think about it. *(He exits.)*

VOICEOVER: Death and flying.

*(*CATHY *enters, carrying two milkshakes to go.* EVELYN *enters.)*

EVELYN: Oh, honey...

CATHY: What?

EVELYN: He's dead.

*(*CATHY *just stands there, not moving for a long beat.)*

CATHY: But...I have the milkshakes.

EVELYN: I have to call people.

(EVELYN *exits.* CATHY *crosses to the right, then to the left, then to the right, then she stops.* JIM *enters and talks to her, but she can't see or hear him.*)

JIM: I just had the most incredible dream. Honey?
I dreamed I was flying, surrounded by light. But it was so real. I could feel this hot...wind on my neck.
The tops of trees were just whizzing past below me.
And, I'm not kidding, the sound of wings! I reached back to rub myself. And that's when I saw the nest and the open mouths. (*He grabs onto something that seems solid at his sides and then bends his head up and back to see what is above him. He realizes that something is clutching him.*
He looks at the audience.) Oh. I get it. Beyond the light.
Angel meat. Noooo.

VOICEOVER: We hear the sound of sirens.

CATHY: Wait a minute.

(ACTOR/ ALIEN *enters, speaks to* CATHY.)

ACTOR/ ALIEN: We hear the sound of sirens.

CATHY: *Not yet.*

(CATHY *and* EVELYN *are looking at a plate of Jello with fruit salad suspended in it.*)

EVELYN: Good. Eat that. We don't have any more room in the refrigerator.

CATHY: I was just looking at it. Wondering how Judy's mom got it to...

EVELYN: Yeah. It's all even — the cherries and the grapes didn't go to the....I don't know what to do next. We used to be nomads, you know.

CATHY: Women did all the work.

EVELYN: But it kept your mind off everything. Your husband says it's time to leave and you leave. The baby you lost, whatever, you have to leave it. Someone is always making you do something. You don't have to find a reason to go on.

CATHY: What's that? *(Sound of far-off arguing)* Judy and her mother.

EVELYN: This whole street—it's practically all women now. I thought my father knew everything when I was a girl. And then the president.

CATHY: I thought you knew everything when I was little, Mom.

EVELYN: Oh, let's not lie—after everything we've seen. *(She exits.)*

CATHY: *(Sensing something)* Somebody there? *(No answer)* Somebody there? *(ERIC enters.)*

ERIC: Whatsup, Mom.

CATHY: Oh my God!

(CATHY stands—afraid to touch him—a long beat.)

CATHY: Are you all right? *(ERIC nods.)* Grandpa's dead, Eric. And you weren't even here.

ERIC: I know.

CATHY: How did you get here?

ERIC: I called Kim for money.

CATHY: Kim?

ERIC: Kim. You know—Dad's...girlfriend.

CATHY: You didn't talk to your dad?

ERIC: I thought he'd be mad. *(Pause)* You look mad, too.

CATHY: You don't care about anybody but yourself!!

(EVELYN enters.)

EVELYN: Oh—

ERIC: Hi, Grandma.

CATHY: So Kim knew where you were and didn't call me?!!!

ERIC: Only for twelve hours or so. Mom, give her a break—she's pregnant and she's only eighteen, and—

CATHY: Oh, big deal—that's how old I was when I had you, and you turned out just— (CATHY *stops, unable to say "just fine".)*

ERIC: It fuckin' pisses me off!! This fuckin' life!!!

EVELYN: Eric, for crying out loud!!

ERIC: *Gramma, get off my fuckin' back!!!*

EVELYN: *(Overlapping) Eric, how can you talk to your grandmother that way!*

ERIC: *(Overlapping) Leave me the fuck alone!*

EVELYN: *(Overlapping) As long as you live in this house—*

ERIC: *(Overlapping) Am I in this family or not?!!*

CATHY: Wait—Wait— Come here. Both of you. There's something.

EVELYN: What?

ERIC: What, Mom?

CATHY: Something—a moment of...peace.

VOICEOVER: Oh— She finally has a Moment.

ERIC: Where?

EVELYN: I want that.

CATHY: Listen.

EVELYN: I hear the traffic on the interstate.

ERIC: I hear a TV.

CATHY: Listen.

EVELYN: I can't hear anything.

CATHY: Something— It's going. It's gone. Nevermind.

ERIC: What was it?

CATHY: I don't know. I just had this feeling that everything—

EVELYN: Will be all right? How can it?

ERIC: No shit.

CATHY: No, that everything *is* all right.

ERIC: Well, that's fucked, I can tell you that.

EVELYN: Goes double for me. (ERIC *and* EVELYN *exit into the house.*)

CATHY: *(After a long beat)* Dad?

(ALIEN *crosses right up to* CATHY *and looks at her face, particularly her eyes. He is puzzled by the tears he sees there.*)

CATHY: Daddy?

(CATHY *listens for* JIM, *decides she's missed him somehow, starts for* ERIC's *bag. Seeing that she's disturbed,* ALIEN *gets it for her and hands it to her—she takes it as if it were levitated, and exits.* ALIEN *tries to feel the moment of peace with his hands—can't find it, gives up.*)

VOICEOVER: We hear the sound of sirens. *(No objection—* ALIEN *makes siren sound.*)

(CATHY *and* EVELYN *stand on a hill overlooking Formican. We hear the sound of sirens.*)

CATHY: Look! It's Elvis Presley flying overhead.

EVELYN: Yeah. He's really burning.

CATHY: Uh-oh.

EVELYN: He'll catch those shake shingles — they'll go like — (*Snaps her fingers*) — that.

CATHY: They should've used fake ones like Denny's.

EVELYN: Is that the Pizza Hut that just went up?

CATHY: No, Mom, that's the somethingorother church.

EVELYN: Too near the mall. Big mistake.

CATHY: (*Just noticing*) The dumpster at Roy Rogers! Look, it's caught the roof!

EVELYN: There goes the Flea Market! Those booths go up fast.

CATHY: The wind is carrying it. Look! All the recliners are smoldering.

EVELYN: It's getting very close — They won't be able to keep it out. They won't be able to keep it out. Look at the sparks —

CATHY: Down the air conditioning vents.

EVELYN: Only a matter of time.

CATHY: Flaming gas running into the redwood flower boxes.

EVELYN: It's surrounded.

CATHY: It's glowing from the inside. It went up so fast.

EVELYN: The mall is burning.

CATHY: The mall is burning.

(JUDY *enters, carrying a small paper bag. She takes round ice cream sandwiches out and gives one to* EVELYN *and* CATHY.)

JUDY: Have a Dilly Bar.

EVELYN: (*Sudden realization — the Dairy Queen has burned.*) Not the Soft Serve?

JUDY: Yes, it just blew up. Jagger helped it along. I wonder where he got the money for the gas. (JUDY *and* CATHY *give each other a sidelong glance, then turn back to watch the fire.*)

JUDY: *(To* CATHY*)* I was hoping you could get past your pain into Despair and/ or Terror.

CATHY: You're a fine one to talk.

JUDY: Despair and Terror are intolerable.

CATHY: Yes, they lead to action. Pain is gentle. Pain is the River of Life, and you can ride it to the Sea.

JUDY: You are very introspective And somewhat articulate. You are On to Yourself. *(Pause)* You'd better eat your Dilly Bar.

CATHY: Alright. Thank you.

JUDY: Is that all you've got to say? Alright. Thank you?

CATHY: Where are the kids?

JUDY: *(Points down at the site of the fire)* Disneyland.

(JUDY *gives them each sunglasses to wear.*)

JUDY: For the glare. *(They put the sunglasses on and become* ALIENS.*)*

ALL: *(In relief)* Ahhhhh.

EVELYN/ ALIEN: That's better.

(CATHY/ALIEN *talks to audience — as she does,* ERIC/ALIEN *enters and "shows" the kitchen chair from the beginning of the play and sets it near her. He waits while she talks.*)

CATHY/ ALIEN: There were so many Formicans long ago. Fifteen erts ago I lived with a small group. Their culture was complex, yet strangely intangible, and the artifacts are a constant source of...wonder. *(About the chair)* I used to know what this was for. Several of these survived. *(She and the* ERIC/ALIEN *look quizzically at the chair, then at the audience.)*

CATHY/ALIEN *&* JUDY/ALIEN *sing — the song* JUDY *sang as a lullabye at the end of Act One. After a few lines of the song,* JERRY *enters and spreads newspapers on the floor. He lies down on them, takes out a pistol, checks to see if it's loaded and puts the barrel into his mouth — he pauses. The* ALIENS *try to soothe him with the lullabye, even though he can't see them.)*

JUDY/ ALIEN: *(Sings)*
O dinosaur light,
How death becomes you,
And oozes from you,
Red as Mars.
O dinosaur light,
The sky is turning,
Each night you're burning,
With the stars.

The dream of the screendoor,
The dream of the stoop,
The dream of the clothesline,
The dream of the hoop,
The dream of the dirt road,
The dream of the bird,
The dream of the big tree,
The dream of the word.

O crocodile night,
You've always been there,
In the thin air,
Or on the dune.
O crocodile night,
You're always waiting,
Tonight you're mating
With the moon.

Goodnight,
Goodnight,
Goodnight,
Silence—

Goodnight.

(JUDY/ALIEN & CATHY/ALIEN *exit, tiptoeing to be quiet.* JERRY *has fallen asleep with the pistol in his mouth. He snores contentedly.*)

VOICEOVER: Goodnight.

END OF PLAY